I0212097

FAITH AND REASON

CONSIDER CHRISTIANITY VOLUME 3

ELGIN L HUSHBECK JR.

Energion Publications
Gonzalez, Florida
2021

Copyright © 2021, Elgin L. Hushbeck, Jr. All Rights Reserved.

Scripture taken from the Holy Bible: International Standard Version® Release 2.0. Copyright © 1996-2013 by the ISV Foundation. Used by permission of Davidson Press, LLC. ALL RIGHTS RESERVED INTERNATIONALLY.

Cover Image: Adobe Stock # 180671547

ISBN: 978-1-63199-744-0
eISBN: 978-1-63199-745-7
Library of Congress Control Number: 2021933304

Energion Publications
P. O. Box 841
Gonzalez, FL 32560

energion.com
pubs@energion.com

To

Larissa Munz

My daughter

TABLE OF CONTENTS

ACKNOWLEDGMENTS

This book was several decades in the making and is based on hundreds of conversations I have had over the years. I want to thank all of these people, both supporters and critics alike. All influenced my thinking, either giving me new insights or have allowed me to test and hone existing ideas and beliefs. Some of these are quoted anonymously in this book; all were important. Thank you.

I also need to thank my wife, who has been very patient with me and shared my struggles to learn and live faith. We have been through this journey together, and this book could not have been written without her love and support. She is my wife, my friend, and my partner.

I also want to thank Helen Wisniewski for her detailed and thoughtful feedback on an early draft. Finally, I want to thank my friends at Energion, my editor Chris Eyre, whose critical but helpful eye resulted in some valuable suggestions and improvements. Then, of course, my publisher Henry Neufeld for his kind support and encouragement over the years.

PREFACE

This book was a long time in the making. Growing up as an atheist and only becoming a Christian in my twenties, the issues discussed here have long been of interest to me. I grew up with a love of science and engineering. Growing up in the 1960s, hope and turmoil surrounded me. There was the hope of Kennedy's challenge to reach the moon by the end of the decade and the turmoil caused by the growing conflict in Vietnam. Also, the combined hope and turmoil of the civil rights movement, the hope of a better America, and the growing turmoil to achieve it.

In the midst of all this, I wondered how it was people could hold such different opinions. Differences of opinion occurred, not only with the Vietnam war and the civil rights movement but also with the space program. Something I saw as exciting and important, others saw as a waste of money. Thus, for me, there have always been at least two questions for every issue. How do people disagree, and why do people disagree? Since I am now in my mid-sixties as I write this, in one sense, this book is at least fifty-plus years in the making.

Becoming a Christian added whole new dimensions to my thinking about how you know what you know; why do you believe what you believe? Later, I would learn these questions were part of the philosophical study of epistemology. As I struggled with these questions, my understanding continued to grow and develop. As I would have discussions with people who disagreed, these questions were always there in the background. Sometimes they came to the foreground as I was more interested in how someone came to their current view than the view itself.

When I started writing, again, these questions often came up as I tried to make convincing arguments, not just to those who already agreed, but especially to those who disagreed. It is the latter who are the main focus of my first two books in this series, *Evidence for the Bible* and *Christianity and Secularism*[1]. To write these books, I had to reach a better understanding of why I believed and how I could communicate this to others.

Making this book somewhat different from the first two, the primary audience here are fellow Christians. This is not to say that non-Christians would not benefit from reading this book; they would, just as Christians can benefit from the first two books in the series. It is just that they are not the main focus.

After completing the first two volumes, I immediately began writing this book with the intention of having it published in a timely fashion. The first draft was nearly completed, and my publisher was looking forward to it, but the more I thought about it, the more I did not think I was ready to write about faith. I began praying for a better understanding. Shortly after this, I discovered my wife had been praying for the same thing, so we began praying together for faith. Some very difficult years followed. Our faith was both severely tested and confirmed many times. It also deepened as nearly 15 years passed.

While I never really forgot about this volume, much of the memory of what I had written did fade. I wrote several other books during this period and began work on a book about truth. In 2019, I began to think more about finishing the third volume when I stumbled across a printed copy of my first draft. I did not remember that I had written so much. I searched and found an electronic version and so began to finish it.

---

1   Elgin Hushbeck, *Evidence for the Bible*, (Gonzalez, FL: Energion Publications, 2007)
     Elgin Hushbeck, *Christianity and Secularism*, (Gonzalez, FL: Energion Publications, 2007)

There were a lot of changes. While what I had written was not wrong, neither did it reflect my current understanding. Some parts I discarded. Other parts needed to be rewritten or expanded into a broader discussion or with changes in emphasis. As a result, there are three parts to this book. Part one discusses how, as Christians, we should think about faith and reason, how the two fit together, and how to deal with them when they conflict. Along the way, I deal with some common criticisms concerning faith and reason.

Part two focuses on rational thinking and how to avoid errors. These are not strictly Christian issues or even religious ones. A generic course in critical thinking will cover much of the same material but from a secular perspective. I have taught many such classes. Here I use a Christian focus to take examples from the Bible, fellow Christians, and critics. Part three deals with the impact of Part I and II on how we live our faith.

The resulting book is not a book I could have written when I first started it nearly 15 years ago. Strangely, neither is it a book I could have written now. The reason is that in my first draft, I used many real-life examples. These came from discussions I have had over the years, discussions I had long since forgotten until I reread the first draft. Many of these were on internet services or even pre-internet services that have long since shut down.

There are pros and cons to using these examples. On the pro side, these are real-life examples; they represent real arguments made by real people. While in some places, I summarized some of the more detailed arguments for the sake of space, and in some cases, the reader's interest, normally these are in their own words. Some of the more well known and commonly used arguments only have a general attribution to a group. But where the argument appears as a quote, I am quoting a particular individual and using their own words with changes only for grammar and spelling.

For most of the examples, I have chosen to use a fake first name to be effectively anonymous. Thus the quote at the beginning of Chapter One is attributed simply to Bob. I did this so the reader would know these are actual arguments from real people. Still, being anonymous keeps the focus on the argument, not on the person making the argument.

A few quotes are from identified individuals, people who have published works. I did this mainly because I did not think people would believe some of these were real examples without a reference. Still, the main goal here has been to highlight errors, not individuals.

As for the cons of using these examples, since no one can discuss everything with everyone, there is a focus on the discussions' subject matter. This reflects the discussion in which I have been involved. Still, this should not be taken as a book on how these people/groups are wrong. The errors and problems addressed in this book occur among all people and all groups. Thus, examples of errors I use come from both Christians and non-Christians; they come from groups I agree with and groups with whom I disagree.

You will probably see arguments from groups with which you agree and disagree. You may even see arguments you have used. Still, do not take the use of these errors as arguments against the group or position itself. Again, these errors occur among all groups and all sides. One hope I have is that this book challenges you. Everyone is prone to these errors, including me. The focus here, particularly in Part II, is on thinking correctly about faith issues, not which group is right or wrong. I do that in other books.

Finally, when writing a book like this, some will assume I am setting myself up as the standard. Nothing can be further from the truth. Particularly in Part II, writing this book has been both a difficult and very humbling experience. Correctly thinking in a way that seeks the truth takes constant vigilance. I fall victim to these problems like everyone else. While finishing this book, more than once, I had to rewrite a passage to avoid an error I made in thinking. Often this was an error I had discussed elsewhere in the book. My editor then made additional and very helpful suggestions. Hopefully, I got all of them, but I am pretty certain a few remain. It does show, however, that seeking the truth is a process. It is something we must work at continually. As Christians, seeking truth should always be our goal. To seek truth is to seek God. Jesus said,

"I am the way, the truth, and the life." (John 14:6)

Part I
Faith and Reason

CHAPTER I

HOW DO WE KNOW
WHAT WE KNOW

"What is truth?" (Pontius Pilate, John 18:38)

It is interesting how people look at the same evidence and arrive at radically different viewpoints, is it not? — Bob

I t was a common response and one that I seem to get frequently in one fashion or another. I was in a discussion with an acquaintance. Let's call him Bob, and I had just finished indicating what I believed to be several things I thought were problems with his beliefs. Rather than showing me where I was wrong, Bob just remarked on how people reach different conclusions as if that was a substantive response. Not only was he avoiding the problems I raised, but he was also in effect, attacking the fundamental notion that the evidence can determine truth.

In many respects, Bob's response was very similar to that of Pontius Pilate. John 18 records how the Jewish leaders brought Jesus before Pilate to be crucified, yet, Pilate was not their puppet; he was the Roman governor after all. Instead of simply sentencing Jesus as the Jewish leaders had hoped, Pilate began questioning him about the charge he claimed to be king of the Jews.

This could have been a difficult question. Jesus, as the Christ, was king of the Jews. If he answered yes, Pilate would have valid grounds to execute him for challenging Roman rule. Yet, Jesus was not one to be easily trapped. His reasons for being there went far beyond the mere political issue of who was the current ruling authority, so he was careful to point out he was not, in fact, challenging the Roman rule over the Jews. Instead, he said, "My kingdom does not belong to this world."

Pilate, seeing a possible opening, seized on the reference to "my kingdom," proclaiming, "So you are a king?" to which Jesus replied, "You say that I am a king. I was born for this, and I came into the world for this: to testify to the truth. Everyone who is committed to the truth listens to my voice." Pilate was exasperated. Seeing this was getting him nowhere, he asked rhetorically, "What is truth?" and left.

Pilate's question was not a serious one about the nature of truth. Instead, as a rhetorical one, like most such statements, it was simply a way of sidestepping an issue with which he didn't want to deal. Pilate wanted to find a legitimate reason for crucifying Jesus, to avoid the appearance of simply doing the Jewish leaders' bidding. Pilate became frustrated when Jesus instead talked of truth. His reply was, essentially, why have such a discussion when no one really knows what truth is? The same can be said about the acquaintance with whom I was talking.

Bob's claim that different people can look at the same evidence and come away with completely different conclusions is, of course, true, and it happens all the time. But why is that? Is it because evidence itself is unreliable as a means of determining truth? Is the reason people reach different conclusions a problem with the evidence? If so, then Bob's response was a valid means of rejecting the evidence I had given him. After all, Bob was claiming the evidence was unreliable. Why bother responding to it if it was unreliable?

There is, however, another possibility. When two people look at the same evidence and reach different conclusions, the problem may not be with the evidence; the problem may be with one or even both of the people. In short, one or both could be wrong, something that happens all the time. More importantly, not only is this a different view of the source of the problem, the consequences of this view are different as well. Rather than dismissing the evidence and discouraging discussion, this view encourages the search for further evidence and continued discussion to uncover and correct those errors. This latter view is the basis of much of modern life. We have legal systems based on the evaluation of evidence rather than trial by combat or the casting of lots. Our very concept of the universe itself is based on the scientific method emphasizing evidence, testing, and verification.

As a side note, as it turned out, Bob never did address the problems I raised.

CAN WE KNOW THE TRUTH?

While Pilate may not have meant his question to be a serious one, it is nevertheless important. Can we know what is true? Can we determine what is true and what is false by using evidence and reason? These questions are far deeper, more complex, and important than they may at first seem. One of the foundations of western civilization is the belief that reality can be discovered by looking at the evidence around us. Using reason, we can draw logical conclusions from that evidence. In other words, we can take what we know, and by using reason, learn things we did not know before.

Western civilization answered these questions in a way that resulted in the scientific and technological orientation many now take for granted. However, while we may take it for granted, there are other ways these questions have been answered. Other civilizations have taken different approaches. Many eastern cultures did not look for reality in the world around us but instead sought an inner truth. As a result, while they have very old and highly developed civilizations, they made few scientific advances. While these cultures made many discoveries (e.g., printing), these did not have anywhere near the same impact as they did when introduced into the west (e.g., printing press).

The idea that we can know what is true with some degree of certainty formed the basis of western civilization. This notion is increasingly coming under attack, especially outside of the natural sciences. One discussion I had with a software engineer is pretty typical; let's call her Susan. When the subject of religion and morality came up in the discussion, she stated that we could not know the truth. But she did not stop there and went on to claim there was no such thing as absolute truth. "I don't believe in absolutes," Susan said, "just a lot of grays."

There are two main problems with such statements. First, to say there are no absolutes is itself an absolute statement. Even saying you cannot know anything about morality is to know something about morality. As a result, if taken as a general statement, it contradicts itself and is self-refuting. Even if we ignore that, there is still the second problem, one which a simple question quickly demonstrated. Contrary to her statement, Susan did believe in absolutes. In fact, not only did she believe that moral values exist as absolutes, she believed she could know these were absolutes.

In our normal day-to-day life, Susan is correct, things are often very complex, and there are "a lot of grays." Rarely are issues so straight forward and clear cut so as to be black and white. Thus, when seeking to answer whether there are absolutes, typical real-life examples are rarely good candidates. For example, ask about absolutes with "is theft wrong," and someone will probably come back with, "What about stealing a loaf of bread to feed your starving child?"

As such, the question we ask must be both stark and well defined to remove any possible 'What ifs.' The question I asked Susan was one I learned from one of my philosophy professors. "Is it absolutely wrong to torture babies for fun?" Suddenly all the grays were gone, and she had no trouble agreeing this was absolutely wrong.

In fact, of the hundreds of people I have asked this question, I can only remember one, call him Mike, who said he did not believe this was an absolute because he did not believe in moral absolutes. To his credit, Mike said he was uncomfortable with his answer. I say this was to his credit because while I believe we can know the truth, we do not know all of it. As I will discuss later, all systems of belief have problems, things supporters cannot answer very well, or in this case, that make one uncomfortable. Most people ignore these problems, pretending they do not exist. Mike's recognizing the problem with his own views demonstrated he had a good degree of self-analysis, and this was to his credit.

EVIDENCE AND TRUTH

The idea that we can get truth from evidence and reason is not something complex or difficult. We do it all the time. For example, let's say, one morning you wake up to find the ground covered with a fresh blanket of snow. You know, last night before you went to bed, there was no snow on the ground, so you know it snowed sometime last night. This is a simple example of drawing a conclusion based on evidence. You did not see it snow but concluded it had from the evidence.

There are other possibilities. For example, aliens could have come and beamed the snow onto your neighborhood, so it only looked just like it had snowed. Yet, we can easily reject such "possibilities" as unlikely and probably do not even consider them. They do not detract from our ability to say, "it snowed last night." Your neighbor's suggestion that aliens were responsible would probably cause you to question their ability to reason and wonder if it is time to move.

Thus, in many situations, we take it for granted that a rational evaluation of the evidence can lead to the truth. We base our entire legal system on this ability. As an example of just how important we think evidence is, consider the following. You have spent the entire day (10:00 AM - 8:00 PM) with a group of friends at an amusement park. You were never separated from them for more than 10 minutes and show up on numerous security cameras around the park throughout the day. At 2:15 PM that day, a robbery was committed in a city that is a 2-hour drive from the amusement park.

The next day the police arrest you because you drive a car similar to one reported near the crime. The police have no other evidence linking you to the crime. Do you want to be judged based on the evidence or some other basis at your court appearance? Would you be more comfortable knowing the judge was an expert on evaluating evidence or that the judge ignored the evidence? Would you rather have a judge determined guilt by having the defendant spin a wheel marked "Guilty" and "Not Guilty?" Clearly, in such a situation, most people would want to be judged by the evidence.

Still, Bob's statement at the beginning of this chapter, in which different people can look at the same evidence and reach completely different conclusions, is undoubtedly true. If this were not the case, there would never be such a thing as a hung jury. How can this be if evidence is so reliable? There are three main reasons. The first, as suggested earlier, is the use of faulty reasoning. Some very common ways of thinking about things are logically unsound and can easily lead to false conclusions. We will look at this in more detail in Part II.

The second reason comes from a problem with evidence. It is not a problem inherent in the evidence itself, but in the simple fact that rarely do we have all the evidence or even as much as we would like. This is the basis of a lot of crime fiction, where everything seems to point to an innocent person until the discovery of a key piece of evidence, exonerating them and pointing to the guilty party. It is not so much a problem with evidence but rather the lack of it, and ultimately it is still the evidence that settles the issue. Imagine the climactic moment at the end of a crime drama. When confronted with a key piece of evidence exonerating the main character, the judge said, "It is interesting how people look at the same evidence and arrive at radically different viewpoints, is it not? I still find you guilty."

Sometimes the evidence we do have is hard to interpret or does not point to definite conclusions. But problems stemming from the lack of evidence do, at least in theory, have a solution: find more evidence. In fact, a large part of science is the quest for new evidence. The third problem is more difficult.

SOURCES OF KNOWLEDGE

The final reason people reach different conclusions is that evidence and reason are not the only sources of knowledge. There are several ways sources of knowledge can be classified. The most important for our discussion are critical/uncritical and objective/subjective. Critical/uncritical refers to whether the information is just accepted or whether it comes from some testing.

It is important to distinguish between being critical and criticizing. Being critical, as we are using it here, means to test and question. To criticize means to call into question negatively. In short, when we test something to see if it is true or false, we are critical. Whereas, when pointing out problems with a position, we are criticizing. This is a very important distinction as some people are uncomfortable with a critical approach to the Bible. They incorrectly see it as somehow criticizing God. However, this is not the case, and as we will see in the next chapter, the Bible tells us to be critical.

A good example of uncritical information is tradition. Tradition is passed on with little or no critical examination and normally received without question. It is important to note here this does not mean that tradition is therefore wrong, only that it is untested. We can test tradition, but if we do and reach a conclusion, it is no longer considered tradition. If we test a tradition about events and reach a conclusion they occurred, they would no longer be tradition but history. If, on the other hand, we concluded they did not happen, then they would be considered legend or myth.

The other way of approaching sources of knowledge is to see them as either objective or subjective. Objective knowledge is based on things others can examine. Subjective knowledge is based on things to which only the individual has access. For example, traditions come down to us from others and thus are objective. Others can also ask about those traditions and learn about them. Only we, however, experience our feelings. While we can tell others about our feelings either through our words or actions, only we experience them. As a result, feelings are subjective.

Another type of subjective knowledge is insight, the knowledge that comes suddenly and seemingly from nowhere. While the introductory section of science textbooks describe the scientific method as a great tool for understanding the world around us, science is by no means restricted to this. Many significant advances in science have come, not from the scientific method but rather, from insight. One well-known example is F. A. Kekule's "discovery" of benzene's structure through a vision of a snake chasing its tail.

While inspiration is similar to insight, it differs because the source is known (or believed to be known) and can be natural or supernatural. Since some do not believe in the supernatural, not all will accept supernatural inspiration as an actual knowledge source. However, many who accept the existence of the supernatural have little problem believing in supernatural inspiration. Still, inspiration is not just supernatural; it is not just God speaking through apostles and prophets. One can be inspired by a great work of art or a beautiful landscape.

Even for supernatural inspiration, there is still a wide range of beliefs and many ways Christians understand it. Inspiration is not generally seen as God speaking in an audible voice. Even in the Bible, such manifestations of God are rare. Rather inspiration is usually seen as something much more subtle. Inspiration is more God leading or influencing. Phrases like 'God spoke to my heart' are common. Even for something like the Bible's inspiration, many views exist. They range from something akin to dictation to a much looser direction, with many variations in between. Some believe that inspiration demands inerrancy; others don't. Even those whose beliefs are closer to dictation allow for the prophet or apostle's influence, and thus the differences in style and language.

A complete discussion of inspiration would be a book of its own. Here we will focus more on two aspects—God's role as the source and our role as the receiver. In terms of a source, the perspective here will be the historical Christian view that God is all-knowing and cannot lie. As such, God is completely trust-worthy. A different view of God's reliability will not substantially change the overall arguments about faith. This is particularly true when we consider our role, which we will do shortly.

Based on these classifications, tradition is uncritical and objective. Unexamined feelings are uncritical and subjective. Our feelings tested are critical and subjective. Evidence and reason are, by their very nature, critical, and since they are accessible to all, they are also objective. This grouping is summarized in Figure 1.

Sources	Subjective	Objective
Critical	Examined Emotions, Insight, and Inspiration	Reason and Evidence
Uncritical	Unexamined Emotions, Insight, and Inspiration	Traditions

Figure 1 Sources of Knowledge

THE RELIABILITY OF KNOWLEDGE

There would be little question of what is true if all these knowledge sources were always in agreement. Unfortunately, this is not the case. When they differ, how can we tell which is correct? In the case of tradition versus evidence, this is normally not that difficult. Still, even here, it is not always as clear cut and easy as it may at first seem. This is because the evidence is not always complete or conclusive.

Say you have a tradition that says something happened, but there is no evidence that it did. Is the lack of evidence because the tradition is wrong; there is no evidence because it did not happen? Or is the tradition correct, with the lack of evidence due to all the evidence being lost? Did the event happen so long ago that nothing is left except the tradition? Is it because we have some evidence, but it is incomplete and not well understood? A key question sometimes overlooked is how likely is it that evidence would be preserved in the first place?

During the 19th century, many biblical accounts were rejected as unhistorical because there was no evidence to support them. Since then, with the discovery of a lot more evidence, many things once rejected as unhistorical are now known to have occurred.

What about the differences between evidence and feelings? Or even more difficult, what about when the evidence disagrees with inspiration? Before we can come to any conclusions, we must first introduce two more considerations: clarity of perception and accuracy. Clarity of perception relates to how well we can identify the information. Since either evidence exists or doesn't, there is little question about its clarity for most evidence. In the example where we concluded that it had snowed, there was no question there was snow on the ground where none existed the night before. This evidence was clear.

The accuracy of the evidence relates to how reliably the evidence points to the conclusion we are trying to draw. Is it a 100 percent indicator? 90 percent? Lesser? Again, to use our snow argument, the existence of fresh snow where none existed the night before is directly related to whether it had snowed. This is a very accurate indicator. Thus, our snow argument is both clear and accurate, and therefore, there is little doubt about the conclusion.

On the other hand, when trying to decide if a person's recovery from a difficult medical condition was a miracle, the mere fact of recovery is not as closely related. People recover from medical conditions all the time, and not all recoveries are miracles. So the relationship between evidence of recovery and the conclusion of miracle is not as accurate. More evidence is needed, evidence such as a particular type of illness or likelihood of recovery.

Complex psychological issues aside, emotions are also very clearly perceived. We normally have very little trouble knowing if we are happy, sad, frightened, or angry. Since emotions are subjective, they are not very accurate indicators of the outside world. Sometimes, our emotional responses can be completely counter to objective reality. Nearly everyone has, at one time or another, felt anger at someone over a given situation, only to discover later that they were the ones at fault. As a result, emotions, while being clearly perceived, are not accurate indicators of reality.

Very much the same can be said for insight. When we receive a sudden insight into a matter, we suddenly see it very clearly, yet this insight can still be wrong. A good example of this is Johannes Kepler's insight into the nature of the solar system. While teaching, Kepler had an insight that the (then known) six planets were related to the five platonic solids. This insight ultimately turned out to be wrong. Still, while the insight was wrong, his attempt to confirm it eventually led him to discover the laws of planetary motion that bear his name[2]. So the insight was still beneficial.

On the opposite end of the spectrum would be supernatural inspiration. Most people would consider God to be a very reliable source of information. In fact, from the historical Christian point of view, God can't be wrong. He knows everything and does not lie. Therefore, inspiration from God would have the highest possible accuracy. Yet, many people claim to have received knowledge from God, and these people do not agree. Often they contradict each other. How do we account for this difference if God is so accurate?

For example, a very small minority of Christians believe the King James Version is the only true word of God. Some in this minority believe that God told them that God's only true and perfect word is the King James Version of the Bible. On the other hand, many Mormons claim that God has told them the Book of Mormon is the only perfect word of God, and the KJV has been corrupted. Both groups are sincere about their claims; both cannot be correct. Given the constraint that God cannot lie, then it must be possible for someone to sincerely believe that God has revealed information to them and yet be wrong. In other words, they either did not understand what God said or confused God with some other source, perhaps confusing inspiration with insight or emotion.

---

2   Husbeck, *Evidence for the Bible*, pp. 79-81

Note that in this discussion of inspiration, I am referring only to direct inspiration. This would not include trusting the Bible because one believes it is inspired unless direct inspiration is the basis for that belief. Direct inspiration is subjective, while the question of the Bible's inspiration is, at least to some extent, objective. The issues surrounding the reliability and inspiration of the Bible are the subject of the first volume in this series, *Evidence for the Bible*.

The bottom line is that direct inspiration is not always clearly perceived. Was it actually divine inspiration or something else? Due to this, we must assign inspiration a low clarity. This low clarity of perception should not be taken to mean that the person claiming knowledge from inspiration is somehow unsure about the source. Both KJV-only supporters and Mormons do not doubt their revelation from God. Both are completely certain that God has revealed the truth to them. It is everyone else who must be wrong. Still, both claims cannot be correct. One or both must be wrong. The point here is that even though a person may not doubt they have received knowledge from God, they can still be wrong.

Returning to the reliability of the various sources of knowledge, reliability is the product of clarity of perception and accuracy. We are the most certain about information that is both clear and accurate. As shown in figure 2, the source of knowledge most likely to meet both criteria is evidence.

Sources	Low Accuracy	High Accuracy
High clarity of perception	Emotions, Insight, and Traditions	Reason and Evidence
Low clarity of perception	Innuendo	Inspiration

Figure 2 Sources of Knowledge

TRUTH AND UNCERTAINTY

Even though evidence and reason are the most likely to be reliable, rarely do they ever give us 100 percent certainty.[3] This inability to be certain has led many to question the reliance on evidence and reason, especially in the area of religion. Here 99 percent certainty is often seen as 1 percent doubt, and any amount of doubt is seen as too much when it comes to our eternal destiny. A person I was talking with once asked, "How can you claim to base your Bible on the evidence when you are one fallible, finite, and imperfect man? Where does evidence end, and God's sovereignty in preservation begin?"

Nor is this view only limited to the fundamentalist. For many atheists, the idea of God is so different from everything else, nothing short of absolute proof is sufficient to conclude God exists or the Bible is true. Any uncertainty, however small, is enough grounds to reject the existence of God. Since such a level of proof is an impossible goal to achieve, they believe their atheism is justified.

Often in discussions with atheists, the issue comes down to one of evidence versus speculation. The evidence pointing to God's existence or the Bible's reliability is rejected. The atheist can always imagine some possible alternative explanation. It is of little importance that there is no evidence to support their imagined alternative. They can conceive the possibility. This speculation about an alternative is reason enough to reject the conclusion pointed to by the evidence. For example, the evidence for the resurrection is very strong. In fact, the resurrection is one of the most documented events in ancient history[4]. Yet, this evidence is written off in favor of speculations about what else might have happened. Maybe someone stole the body, or Jesus

---

3   In fact, as I argue in Volume II, 100 percent certainty is impossible for everything is based, at least to some extent on assumptions that cannot be proved but must just be accepted on faith. See *Christianity and Secularism*, pp. 37-40.

4   Hushbeck, *Christianity and Secularism*, pp. 141-167

survived the crucifixion, or maybe he had a twin brother! None of these alternatives fits the evidence we have, but that does not matter. The speculation is enough to reject the resurrection.

Theists who question reason and evidence in favor of other means of knowledge have their own problems. While they focus on the doubt that remains in conclusions made based on evidence, they ignore the other sources' even greater doubt. Looking only at accuracy, it is certainly true we should trust God over the evidence. God is never wrong; evidence sometimes is. The problem is, however, as we have seen, inspiration is not clearly perceived. In short, while God is never wrong, how can we be sure what we perceived as God speaking to us is actually God speaking to us? Why are we correct to believe our inspiration is from God? Why are those who are also certain about their inspiration wrong?

While it is very difficult to apply any accurate number to these categories, using some sample numbers can help illustrate these concepts. Let's say the evidence supports position A. At the same time, inspiration tells us to reject position A. The evidence is both clearly perceived (95% certain) and very accurate (90% certain). On the other hand, direct inspiration from God is always accurate (100% certain) but not clearly perceived (50% certain). The choice is clear if we look only at the accuracy. Inspiration, at 100% accuracy, is better than the evidence, which is only 90% accurate. Yet when we consider both accuracy and clarity, we get a different story. To get the total reliability, you would multiply the accuracy and clarity. When we do this for the evidence, we multiply 95% (perception) times 90% (accuracy) for a total reliability of 86%. For inspiration, we have 50% times 100% for total reliability of 50%. Thus, while direct inspiration has higher accuracy, because of the uncertainty concerning whether it was inspiration from God, overall, it is not as reliable as evidence.

While relying on evidence does leave some doubt, this really should not be seen as anything new. We live with doubt and uncertainty every day. It is a part of everything we do. There is the adage; nothing is certain except death and taxes. Yet even in these areas, there are uncertainties. Except for those directly facing death or those on death row, few know the time or means of their death, and no one understands all of the tax code. Every time we drive a car, there is a possibility we will be killed in a traffic accident. There is a doubt that you will arrive safely. Yet this doubt does not keep us from driving. While there is a risk, it is so small that people ignore it most of the time, unless they are the parents of teenage drivers.

Risk is just doubt about what will happen. We all, to some extent, weigh the risks and act based on those risks. Some of these decisions will have lifelong effects. When a couple gets married, is there any guarantee the marriage will work out? When a person chooses a career, can they be 100% certain they will be able to get a job in that field ten or twenty years from now? All we do involves uncertainty to one extent or another. It is a part of life. Why should religion be any different?

If there is always some doubt, does that mean we can never really know the truth? It all depends on how one defines "know." As a practical matter, once the uncertainty becomes small enough, we can safely say that we know. For example, many people will claim to know Russia's capital is Moscow, even though the vast majority of them have never been there. While there remains an extremely small possibility it is all a hoax, that there is no such city, most people easily reject such possibilities. They see "Moscow is the capital of Russia" as a true statement. They would claim that this is something they know to be true.

A similar situation exists for error. Once the level of uncertainty reaches a given level, we say that something is in error. For example, say you are a second-grade teacher, and a student comes to class saying they did their homework. On the way to school, they continue, a monster took it from them. I doubt you would have any trouble rejecting their story as untruthful.

TESTS OF TRUTH

How can we tell when something is true or false? There are
no hard and fast rules. Sometimes, the evidence is just so clear
that there is no rational basis for doubt. At other times, things are
not that simple. The following are three tests commonly used to
decide whether or not something is true. None are perfect. None
will work in every case, but they do give us some good guidelines.

Correspondence: It Agrees with Facts

A fact is something that can objectively be said to be true. The
moon orbits the earth. There are 2.54 centimeters in an inch. Both
facts. This is a pretty straightforward test. It was the test Johannes
Kepler used to see if his insight concerning the relationship between
the platonic solids and the orbits of the planets was correct. He
figured out where his model said the planets should be at a given
time. He then checked to see if they were where his model pre-
dicted. His model's predictions were very close, but close was not
good enough. At first, Kepler believed the problem was not with
his theory. Rather, he believed the error was with the measurements
of the position of the planets. So Kepler sought other, more accurate measurements. After years of testing, in the end, he became
convinced that the difference between his theory and the facts was
so great that he had to reject his theory and began looking for an
alternative. The search for this alternative theory led Kepler to his
now accepted laws of planetary motion.

Pragmatic: It Works When Tested

The correspondence test works great when we test things that
can easily be compared to reality, but that is not always possible.
The pragmatic test equates what works to what is true. This test
is good when testing things that cannot be examined directly, but
the results or effects are visible. For example, much of Einstein's
theory of relativity could not be tested directly. However, based on

the theory, scientists were able to make some predictions they could test. As the number of such successful tests grew, it showed that Einstein's theory worked and came to be seen as correct.

Coherence: It Fits in With Other Accepted Truths

This test checks to see how a theory or claim fits in with other things believed to be true. In other words, based on what we already believe to be true, is this what we would expect to see. Often, we use this test when determining the level of evidence we require for a given claim. For example, say we know the Acme Car Company makes very fast cars. A friend who knows cars tells us that their newest model is the fastest commercially made car ever produced. Given this knowledge, we are very likely to believe them. On the other hand, if we think Acme makes average cars that are overrated, our friend's claim is likely to be met with skepticism.

This last example reveals a simple fact that accounts for many disagreements: It generally takes more evidence to get us to change a position than to hold on to a position. This shows up in confirmation bias. Suppose we believe a particular food is unhealthy. We may only require one medical study supporting our belief to conclude it is a fact. On the other hand, it might take several medical studies showing no health risk before we changed our position, and even then, we may not change.

While this third test is very common, as you may have already guessed, it has a serious flaw in that it makes a pretty big assumption. For this test to work, you must assume that what you already accept as true is true. Perhaps one of the clearest biblical examples of this test was the Jew's rejection of Jesus as the Messiah because he did not fit their concept of the Messiah.

For a great many 1st century Jews, the Messiah was viewed as a king in the line of David, who would assume power and throw out the hated Romans. At the Triumphal Entry, the crowd shout, "Hosanna!" and "How blessed is the one who comes in the name of the Lord," a quotation of Psalm 118:26. They also added, "the

King of Israel," demonstrating the political goals they had for the
Messiah. When Jesus turned out not to be the type of Messiah
they wanted and expected, rather than question their concept of
Messiah, they rejected Jesus.

What is truly amazing is how the coherence test, even with
its problems, is sometimes allowed to overrule the other tests. For
example, John 11 records Jesus' greatest miracle before his death
and resurrection, raising Lazarus from the dead. Upon hearing of
this, the Sanhedrin did not discount the power of this evidence
concerning Jesus's identity. They said,

> What are we going to do? This man is performing many
> signs. If we let him go on like this, everyone will believe in him,
> and the Romans will come and destroy both our Temple and
> our nation." (John 11:47-8)

Yet, instead of taking this as evidence that Jesus was who he
claimed to be, this evidence itself became an additional problem. As
a result, not only did they plan to kill Jesus (John 11:53), "the high
priests planned to kill Lazarus, too, since he was the reason why so
many of the Jews were leaving to believe in Jesus." (John 12:10-11).

WHAT IS TRUTH?

Was Pilate correct to question truth? Can we ever really know
what is true? Sure! Despite the questions raised by some, we can
know a great deal. In fact, the view we cannot know anything is
self-refuting, for it is a statement that itself claims to be true.

Setting aside some of the deeper philosophical issues,[5] a simple
definition of truth is nothing more than that which conforms to
reality. We can know we are part of the reality in which we exist.
Even if we live in an artificial reality, as in the movie The Matix, we
can still know the part of the artificial reality where we live. Such
considerations would affect the nature of the reality in which we
live. It would not affect things such as the location of our favorite

---

5   I will be dealing with the various philosophical views of truth and the
     issues surrounding them in a future book on truth.

restaurant. Other parts of the reality can be discovered either by the informal means of our experience or the more formal means of study, through subjective means such as inspiration or objective means of evidence. We can reach conclusions about the reality around us based on emotions or reason. The simple fact is everyone uses each of these sources of information (with the possible exception of supernatural inspiration) to varying degrees when coming to conclusions about the reality around us.

The existence of disagreements does not mean that truth is unknowable. Say I were to claim that Abraham Lincoln was president during WWI. In contrast, someone else claimed he was president during the Civil War. This disagreement would not be evidence we cannot know when Lincoln was president. It would be a simple matter to demonstrate that, in this case, I was wrong. In short, the fact that there are disagreements does not demonstrate that something is unknowable. The existence of disagreements only shows that there are disagreements.

In drawing any conclusions about disagreements, we must investigate the reasons for them. In some cases, disagreements are the result of a lack of evidence. In such cases, the matter is unknowable, at least until we discover more evidence. As such, we may never know the identity of Jack the Ripper. Often, however, there are other reasons. There is the likelihood that one or both sides are unfamiliar with the evidence that does exist. There is the possibility that they base their conclusions on faulty reasoning. Then there is a possibility that one side is ignoring the evidence and relying on some other source such as emotions or tradition.

Finally, when it comes to religion, some believe that everything is unknowable and must be so. Religion is the realm of faith, not knowledge, and thus is somehow different than the rest of the human experience. Religion is simply a matter of belief in which evidence and reason play no part. For these people, the statement, "Caesar Augustus ruled Rome during the last part of the 1ˢᵗ century B.C.," is seen as a historical statement reflecting reality. Yet, somehow the statement "Jesus was born during the reign of Caesar

Augustus" is only a statement of belief outside the realm of what can be known. Still, both are historical. Both have strong evidence upon which to base their validity.

While faith is important to religion and central to Christianity, neither Christianity nor religion are restricted to the realm of faith. We can subject religious truth to many of the same tests for truth used for other realms of the human experience. The same tests can judge biblical passages that purport to recount historical events as they do other documents claiming to be historical. When judged as such, the biblical statement holds up quite well.[6] Not only is truth knowable, but religious truth is knowable. But if so, then what is the role of faith?

---

6   Hushbeck, *Evidence for the Bible*

CHAPTER 2

FAITH AND REASON

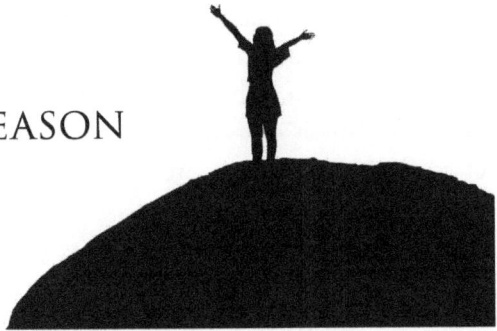

Anything that is not done in faith is sin. (Romans 14:23)

Attempting to respond to the points which you have listed is difficult at best. Clearly we are speaking of a subjective decision based almost exclusively on faith and inspiration from the Holy Spirit. – Harold

I was talking with a man, call him Harold, about the Bible. He claimed that to look at the evidence showed a lack of faith. The evidence, or at least our understanding of it, was fallible. Rather than concentrate on the evidence, we should just have faith in God and the preservation of His word, or at least the particular translation Harold used.[7]

In the last chapter, we examined some of the problems with such claims. Still, Harold's statement raises another issue: are faith and reason even compatible? By looking at the evidence, is one somehow showing a lack of faith? Must one base their decisions only on faith, or only on reason? And, what do we do when faith and reason disagree? Before we can begin to answer such questions, we must better understand what faith is. From a Christian perspective, the key biblical passage on this question is Hebrews chapter 11.

---

7   The man was supporting the KJV-only position which claims that the KJV is not just a good translation of God's word, but is in fact the only real word of God in English and that all other translations are corruptions of God's Word.

WHAT IS FAITH

Hebrews is one of the most complex and beautifully written portions of the New Testament. It is a letter, but not a normal one. It does not have a standard opening identifying the sender and the recipient, which one would normally expect from a 1st-century letter. Rather, it jumps directly into its subject. As a result, and as one might expect, there is disagreement among scholars over 1) who wrote it, 2) to whom they were writing, and 3) the occasion behind the letter. I believe Hebrews was written in the mid-60s, a time of growing tensions in Israel between the Jews and the Romans. In A.D. 64, the Roman Prefect Albinus was recalled for incompetence after only two years of rule. His replacement, Florus, was even worse. The Jews were growing increasingly tired of Roman domination, marked by the rule of corrupt leaders. In just a few years, an open rebellion against Rome would break out – a rebellion that would result in the destruction of Jerusalem and the Temple.

In such a climate, many Jews who had embraced Christ's teachings would undoubtedly have been torn between their new faith and their homeland. Some probably felt they were abandoning the faith of their fathers just when they were most needed to oppose the tyranny of Rome.

It was most likely to just such a group of Jewish Christians that the author[8] of Hebrews wrote. He carefully structured this letter as an argument pointing out that following Christ was not rejecting the faith of their fathers, but instead, is fulfilling it. In the early part of the letter, the author describes the position of Christ as both God and man. He describes Jesus' role as our high priest and the Levitical priesthood as a shadow of the true priesthood

---

8   The generally accepted view is that little is known about the authorship
     of Hebrews accept that the traditional view that this letter was written by
     Paul is in error. I do not find the arguments against Pauline authorship
     persuasive and thus believe that Paul most likely authored the letter.
     However, whoever wrote the letter, it is clear that their main purpose
     was to focus on and exalt God and thus the question of authorship is not
     critical to understanding the letter.

found in Jesus. Jesus has a better priesthood, a better offering (the heart of the letter), and, therefore, a better result, a result that is accessed by faith.

To the first-century Jew, faith's centrality could easily have been seen as a major departure from Judaism. At that time, Judaism focused on what one did; in short, did one keep the law. Thus, in chapter 11, the author traces the role and importance of faith in the Jewish religion. Starting with Abel, he demonstrates that faith was nothing new but an integral part of Judaism from the very beginning.

As with many good discussions of a topic, the author of Hebrews first defines faith, so there is no doubt concerning what he is talking about,

> Now faith is the assurance that what we hope for will come about and the certainty that what we cannot see exists. By faith our ancestors won approval. By faith we understand that time was created by the word of God, so that what is seen was made from things that are invisible. (Hebrews 11:1-3)

He defines faith as the "assurance" and "certainty" of what we hope for yet do not see. The word translated in the ISV, RSV, and NASB as "assurance" is the Greek word hupostasis (ὑπόστασις), translated in the NIV as "being sure" and in the KJV as "substance." The word has caused some difficulty in translation. It can refer either to a sense of assurance (guarantee, attestation) or the nature of something (substance, essence, foundation). The context here would indicate the former, that faith is the assurance we have that what we hope for will happen. The word translated "certainty" (elenchos - ἔλεγχος) is easier to translate. It refers to verification, evidence, or proof of something and was used in first-century writings when referring to legal proof.

One aspect of this definition is that faith is distinct from belief. Faith is not the belief itself but the sense of confidence we have in what we believe. It is possible to believe something and still not have faith in it (See James 2:19).

For example, helicopters are sometimes used to work on very high voltage lines.[9] A helicopter flies close to the power line. A cable is attached to the power line to equalize the potential between the line and the helicopter. Once that is done, a technician can work on the line. They can even crawl out onto the line, all while the power is still on, without being shocked.

Knowing something about electricity, I understand the basics of the science behind this. We have all seen this in action when we see birds sitting on high voltage wires without being shocked. While I believe it and even understand it, I am not sure how much faith I would have in my belief if I were the one in the helicopter. I am sure there would be some hesitation as I had to reach out and touch an electrical line with tens of thousands of volts going through it. In this case, there would be a distinct difference between my belief that it would work and my faith that it would work.

This difference between belief and faith is also seen in the example the author of Hebrews chooses to clarify his definition: creation. What makes this interesting is that the Bible uses creation as evidence that there is a God. Psalm 19:1 states, "The heavens are declaring the glory of God, and their expanse shows the work of his hands." In Romans 1:18-20, Paul writes:

> For God's wrath is being revealed from heaven against all the ungodliness and wickedness of those who in their wickedness suppress the truth. For what can be known about God is plain to them, because God himself has made it plain to them. For since the creation of the world God's invisible attributes—his eternal power and divine nature—have been understood and observed by what he made, so that people are without excuse.

Thus, the world's creation is used both as an example of faith and a reason to believe in God. While this may at first seem a con-

---

9   Polden, J. (2015, June 16). Electric performance. Retrieved from DailyMail.com: http://www.dailymail.co.uk/news/article-3126209/Man-demonstrates-maintaining-high-voltage-line-half-million-volts-pass-body.html.

flict, actually, the two go together quite well. While by no means universal, the very existence of the universe was seen by many people throughout history as evidence for God's existence. Today, some of the strongest arguments for God's existence are based on the universe and creation.[10]

In his example, the author of Hebrews does not just refer to the creation in general but singles out two aspects. The ISV translates the first one as "time was created by the word of God." The word translated time is the Greek word aionas (αἰῶνας) and means ages. It was used as a way of describing everything. God did not just create, for example, a mountain; he created the mountain as it is, as it was, and as it will be. To say he created the ages is to say that he created everything as it was, as it is, and as it will be. To put this in modern terms is to say that he created the entire universe, including time itself.

The second aspect is that God spoke the universe into existence. The phrase "word of God" here is mistakenly taken by some as referring to Jesus. This is because John's Gospel opens by saying, "In the beginning was the Word." John then goes on to identify "the Word" as Jesus. The problem is that the writers of John and Hebrews are using different Greek words. While John used the Greek word logos (λόγος), in Hebrews, the word is rhema (ῥῆμα).

Rather than pointing back to the Gospel of John, which probably had not been written at the time Hebrews was written, the author is pointing back to Genesis. In Genesis, God spoke the universe into creation, such as in Genesis 1:3, "God said, 'Let there be light!' So there was light." The author of Hebrews emphasizes this by saying that what was created by God's command came from nothing. More literally, 'not out of things that appear, were the thing we see created' which the ISV translation smooths out to "so that what is seen was made from things that are invisible."

10　Two would be the Cosmological Argument (based on existence of a cause and effect universe) and the Teleological Argument based on design. The Cosmological Argument is discussed in *Christianity and Secularism* pp. 59-63, the Teleological is discussed in *Evidence for the Bible*, pp. 100-1

Hebrews is not saying that it is by faith that we believe God created the universe. Rather, by faith, we believe God created the universe by his command and out of nothing. The evidence during the first century was very supportive of the belief that God created the universe. Still, it did not prove that the God of the Bible was the creator or that he created it out of nothing. Of course, one can believe that the universe was created, yet believe some other god than the God of the Bible created it. It is when we go beyond the evidence of a created universe, to hold that it was created by God's command out of nothing as described in the Bible, that faith is required.[11]

Faith is the confidence in a position that goes beyond what we can fully support. Implied in this definition, and more clearly stated elsewhere in the Bible (e.g., James 2:26), faith is the confidence that leads us to act on our beliefs. This aspect of faith is seen in a little child standing on the edge of a pool. They want to jump into the arms of their parent in the pool. The child may believe their parent will catch them, but such a belief does not always lead them to jump. When their belief combines with confidence to the point that actions result (i.e., they jump into their parent's arms), we can say they had faith.

Having defined what is meant by faith, the author of Hebrews then proceeds to illustrate this definition. He does so with a series of examples to flesh out the definition. Each example follows that same general pattern: a belief and confidence that leads to action. These examples fill the rest of the chapter. By faith, Abel offered a better sacrifice (v 4), Noah built the ark (v 7), Abraham left his homeland (v 8), and Moses led the Jews out of Egypt (v 29). All the examples that the author gives are of people who did something because of their faith. As such, we end up with a definition of faith

---

11   The later part of this example has received tremendous support from modern science. According to the Big Bang theory, the universe came into being in a big explosion and that before the explosion there was nothing. So during the first century, that the universe was created out of nothing was a statement of faith, now it is much more a conclusion of science. (See *Evidence for the Bible* pp. 106-114).

as the confidence we have in a position beyond what the evidence supports; it is a belief plus confidence that leads to action.

FAITH WITHOUT REASON?

In the Bible, faith is central to our relationship with God. Hebrews 11:6 states that "without faith it is impossible to please God." Some see this and other statements on the importance of faith as subordinating reason to faith. In other words, the evidence is important if and only if it does not conflict with faith. I have had people tell me it is good if the evidence does not support them because it simply means they have more faith, and the more faith, the better! One person once responded to my claim that we must test based on evidence, "These signs are not of the church. The church needs no signs. It lives by faith."

One problem with such a view is that faith, in and of itself, is meaningless. If someone says, "I have faith," what does that mean? Do they have faith in God? Their spouse? Their doctor? Faith must have an object; you must have faith in something. Even if a person claims to have faith in God, that does not necessarily mean they have faith in the true God.

The key question becomes, you have faith, but faith in what? How do you know that your faith is correctly placed? How do you know the object of your faith is worthy of your faith? Over 900 people put their faith in Jim Jones and followed him to Guyana, and then even to the point of committing suicide at his command. They had faith, but their faith was misplaced. More recently, 39 people had faith that they would be picked up by a spaceship following the Hale-Bott comet and so committed suicide.

Faith without reason is blind faith. Blind faith can still save, but only if placed correctly. The problem is that, since it is blind, there is no way to know until it is too late. If we return to the example of the child and the pool, a rational faith would be like a child, seeing their parent there ready to catch them and trusting in their love. In faith, the child jumps into their waiting arms. Blind faith would be a blindfolded child just picking a pool and jumping in without knowing whether or not anyone was there to catch them. If they happen to pick the pool with their parent, all will be fine. What if they pick an empty one?

One other problem with blind faith is that, in reality, it is practically impossible to achieve. A completely blind faith would mean we have no reason for the choice we make, just faith. Thus, a person who wanted a completely blind faith would randomly choose beliefs and then simply have faith that they were correct. Even the strongest supporters of faith over evidence that I have encountered reject such an approach. What most people mean when they claim faith is more important than evidence refers only to additional evidence. Additional evidence is unimportant, specifically evidence that conflicts with what they already believe.

One way to picture the relationship of faith and reason is to imagine yourself in the middle of a forest clearing. Many have found themselves here before, and numerous paths are leading out of the clearing. Some paths are wide; some are narrow; some well-traveled; some less so. You can go in many possible directions, or you could even cut a new trail no one has been down before. For the sake of this example, there is only one correct way, one way that leads to safety; the rest lead to death. So which way do you choose?

Blind faith would have you randomly pick a direction for no particular reason and then go that way. You could pick a path based on subjective preference (e.g., that way looks nice). You could pick a path based on what others have done, the largest or smallest, depending on whether you want to be with or avoid the crowd. As you look around, you notice what looks to be paving stones that indicate the correct path. As you examine them, they go off in a particular direction. Still, the closer they get to the edge of the clearing, the fewer there are until they disappear completely before reaching the edge. Thus, while the paving stones are evidence of the true path, they don't go all the way.

To get out of the clearing and reach safety, you must do two things 1) pick a path, and 2) have enough faith in your choice to follow it. You can't just stick with the evidence, for the evidence only goes so far. With blind faith, you might pick the correct path, though the odds are against it. The choice most likely to be correct is to pick the path indicated by evidence and then have faith that it is the correct choice such that you follow it.

WHEN FAITH AND REASON CONFLICT

In the example of forest clearing, it is easy to settle any conflict between faith and evidence. In real life, this is not always the case. One could theoretically argue we should always follow the evidence. The problem is, as we have seen, the evidence is not always conclusive or even consistent. In fact, in our understanding of God, we should expect conflicts between faith and reason.

Because of our finite minds, we can never hope to understand fully a God who is infinite. We should expect some aspects of God and what he does to be beyond our comprehension. For example, some people have used what philosophers and theologians call The Problem of Evil as a reason to reject the existence of God. The Problem of Evil boils down to this: If God is all-good and God is all-powerful, he would stop all evil. Since evil exists, God cannot be both all-good and all-powerful. While one could hold to the belief that God exists and yet is not all-good or all-powerful or both, most of the time, this is used to reject belief in God altogether.

The problem of evil is a real problem for theists. In fact, it is probably the most difficult problem theists face. Some good partial answers address a lot of the difficulties raised, but there is no complete answer. To paraphrase one of my professors, if you think you have one, stop reading this book and publish your answer immediately! Until you do, the problem remains.

Still, even though a valid problem, it is not sufficient grounds to reject God's existence. To reject God's existence because of the problem of evil, we would need to be in a position to conclude a good God would not have allowed a particular action. We would, in effect, have to pass judgment on God's decisions. How can we do this? How can we ever hope to understand the workings of an infinite mind from our finite perspective?

Our ability to understand the actions of God is, in a limited fashion, akin to an animal's ability to understand our actions. For example, injured animals cannot understand what we do to help them. All the animal knows is that it has pain and wants to avoid it. No amount of reasoning will allow the animal to understand. As the animal cannot understand our actions, even more so, we cannot understand the actions of God.

Another factor is that all systems of thought of any complexity have problems remaining to be solved and, in fact, might be insolvable. The mere fact there are problems with a particular point of view is not a sufficient reason to reject that view. For a point of view to become untenable, those problems must become significant enough to demonstrate the view is false.

A further consideration is that all world views have problems with evil. While a problem for theists, the alternative positions (agnosticism and atheism) have equally serious, and I would argue greater, problems with evil.[12] Valid consideration must include all sides of such issues. I don't think theists have yet come up with a completely adequate answer for the Problem of Evil. Still, I do believe the answers they give are better than those who reject the existence of God.

Judging the conflicts between faith and reason can be difficult, for there are many factors to consider and no single rule covering all situations. It is interesting that Abraham, considered to be the prime Old Testament example of faith, faced just such a dilemma and the author of Hebrews refers to this in his chapter on faith,

> By faith Abraham, when he was tested, offered Isaac—he
> who had received the promises was about to offer his unique
> son in sacrifice, about whom it had been said, "It is through

---

12 This is because, as described in *Christianity and Secularism*, the very
    concept of good and evil are grounded in morality, and without God
    there is no basis for Morality (see chapter 7).

Isaac that descendants will be named for you." (Hebrews 11:17-18)

Abraham faced a true dilemma of faith. The account in Hebrews refers to the events described in Genesis. God had promised Abraham, he and his wife Sarah would have a son. "You are to name him Isaac. I'll confirm my covenant with him as an eternal covenant for his descendants." (Genesis 17:19). God had promised Abraham a son who would carry on the covenant that God had established with him, and that son had been born under miraculous circumstances, as Isaac was born when Abraham was 100 and Sarah 90 (see Genesis 17:17; 21:5)

Later, probably when Isaac was in his early teens, God tested the faith of Abraham. God said to him, "please take your son, your unique son whom you love—Isaac—and go to the land of Moriah. Offer him as a burnt offering there on one of the mountains that I will point out to you." (Genesis 22:2) How was Abraham to resolve this dilemma? This new command seemed contradictory to what God had told him. Isaac had been born as a promise from God to carry on the covenant. Yet, now God was telling Abraham to sacrifice Isaac as a burnt offering. How could Isaac fulfill what God had promised if he sacrificed him?

The author of Hebrews tells us, "Abraham was certain that God could raise the dead" (Hebrews 11:19). Because of this, Abraham went to the mountain that God had indicated to him, the site where the Temple would later be built in Jerusalem (2 Chronicles 3:1). As he came close, Abraham told his servants to wait until he and the boy returned (Genesis 22:5). As it turned out, God did not have to raise Isaac from the dead. He sent an angel to interrupt the sacrifice at the last moment. God provided a ram for the sacrifice in his place. As the author of Hebrews put it, "and figuratively speaking, he did get Isaac back in this way." (Hebrews 11:19)

The word translated by the ISV as "certain" is the Greek word *logisamenos* (λογισάμενος), and it means to think in a logical fashion that considers all the evidence. While the two statements of God seemed to conflict, Abraham used reason to solve his dilemma.

This example of reasoning occurs in such a positive fashion in a chapter devoted to faith's importance. Its placement in Hebrews 11 shows it is not wrong to apply reason to issues of faith, nor are faith and reason mutually exclusive. They can and should work together, as we will see in the next chapter.

FAITH AND DOUBT

What then of doubt? In some respects, doubt is the opposite of faith. Jesus says as much when he asked Peter, "You who have so little faith, why did you doubt?" (Matthew 14:31). Doubt functions as a lack of trust, and whereas faith should lead to action, frequently, doubt leads to inaction. A person who intellectually knows that a bridge will support them, but is still reluctant to cross it, is doubting if their knowledge is correct. This doubt, this lack of faith, will keep them from crossing.

Also, like faith, doubt comes in degrees. Certainly, too much doubt is negative. James writes,

> But he must ask in faith, without any doubts, for the one who has doubts is like a wave of the sea that is driven and tossed by the wind. Such a person should not expect to receive anything from the Lord. He is a double-minded man, unstable in all he undertakes. (James 1:6-8)

The context of this passage is asking for wisdom during suffering, the wisdom of what we can learn, and how we can be better people even when we are suffering unjustly. In such cases, doubting there is anything to learn, any wisdom to be found, is negative. It leaves one focused on the suffering itself and its injustice, closing one's mind to learning. "Such a person should not expect to receive anything from the Lord."

While not everyone who has doubts acts like "a wave of the sea that is driven and tossed by the wind," most people have, at some time in their lives, experienced doubts about a major choice or decision—during that time where they were stuck, going back and forth, unable to reach a conclusion such that this description rings true.

While too much doubt is a problem, doubt itself is both natural and to be expected. In fact, while too much doubt is a problem, as we will see in the next section, so is too little. At first, this may seem odd given the importance of faith, but how could it be otherwise? Proverbs states, "Wisdom is of utmost importance, therefore get wisdom, and with all your effort work to acquire understanding" (4:7), and "Learn diligently, and listen to words of knowledge." (23:12). Implied in these statements that we should seek knowledge and wisdom is that our current knowledge is incomplete. If you know everything, there is no need to seek knowledge. We do not know everything, and so, of course, we will have doubts.

In light of this, we should not be surprised to see Jude writing, "Show mercy to those who have doubts." Doubts are normal and natural, and in many ways, a good thing if channeled correctly. Doubts should lead to questions, and questions should spark the search for answers. This is how we learn. It is only when doubts lead to inaction, or worse, paralysis, that there is a problem. This concept of questioning, even questioning God, is built into the very foundation of the Bible's teaching, starting in Genesis with Abraham's questioning of God

In Genesis 15:1, Abram, later to become Abraham, receives a vision from God saying, "Don't be afraid, Abram. I am your shield. Your reward will be very great." Abram did not respond with thanks or even accept what God was telling him. Instead, he pushed back, saying, "Lord GOD, what can you give me since I continue to be childless… Look! You haven't given me any offspring." (Genesis 15:2-3). When God promised Abram the land has an inheritance, he questioned God, asking, "Lord GOD, how will I know that I will inherit it?" (Genesis 15:8)

Later, God made the covenant with Abram, changing his name to Abraham and promising him a son. Abraham "fell to the ground, laughed, and told himself, 'Can a child be born to a 100-year-old man? Can a 90-year-old Sarah give birth?'" (Genesis 17:17)   As a result, he again questioned God, suggesting Ishmael in place of the promised son.

Perhaps the most famous example of Abraham's questioning of God was his negotiations concerning Sodom and Gomorrah. When Abraham found out what God planned to do, he

> approached and asked, "Will you actually destroy the righteous along with the wicked? Perhaps there are 50 righteous ones within the city. Will you actually destroy it and not forgive the place for the sake of the 50 righteous that are found there? Far be it from you to do such a thing—to kill the righteous along with the wicked, so that the righteous and the wicked are treated alike! The judge of all the earth will do what is right, won't he?" (Genesis 18:23-25)

As soon as God agrees to spare the city for the sake of 50 righteous people, Abraham immediately changed the amount, "What if there are five less than 50 righteous ones? Will you bring destruction upon the city because of those five?" (Genesis 18:28) Eventually, Abraham negotiates God down to sparing the city if there are only 10. And yet, even with these questions, Abraham was a man of faith and mentioned prominently in Hebrew 11, the faith chapter, second only to Moses, who was also known to question God on occasion. It should not be too surprising then to discover that Israel means the one who struggles with God.

Nor is this confined to the Hebrew Bible but is found in the New Testament as well. Throughout the Gospels, we see the disciples frequently questioning Jesus. When John the Baptist was in prison, he understandably had his doubts, asking Jesus, "Are you the Coming One, or should we wait for someone else?" (Matthew 11:3).

While crossing the Sea of Galilee, a storm arose, causing the disciples to be afraid, "but Jesus was in the back of the boat, asleep on a cushion. So, they woke him up and asked him, 'Teacher, don't you care that we're going to die?'" (Mark 4:38) Sure, you can argue that they should not have had doubts, but they did, and they were in the very presence of Jesus. How much more likely is it then that we will have doubts? That we have them is to be expected; what is key is what we do with them.

In John Chapter Six, Jesus gives some particularly difficult teaching, and at the end, "When many of his disciples heard this, they said, 'This is a difficult statement. Who can accept it?'" (John 6:66). So many left that Jesus turned to the twelve asking them, "You don't want to leave, too, do you?" Peter replied, "Lord, to whom would we go? You have the words of eternal life. Besides, we have believed and remain convinced that you are the Holy One of God" (John 6:67-69). While Peter may not have understood and struggled with Jesus' teachings at that time, his faith in Jesus himself remained. But even that waivered with the arrest of Jesus, and he ended up denying Jesus three times (Luke 22:54-62).

Following his resurrection, Jesus appeared before the disciples, but of course, Thomas was absent. "So the other disciples kept telling him, 'We've seen the Lord!' But he told them, 'Unless I see the nail marks in his hands, put my finger into them and put my hand into his side, I'll never believe!' (John 20:25). One week later, Thomas got his wish as Jesus appeared before him, and he believed. He is now known as doubting Thomas for this, but that is somewhat unfair. We should remember that all the disciples doubted until Jesus appeared to them. Luke tells us that the women came back from the tomb and reported what they had seen to the remaining eleven disciples. Did they believe these women? No. "What they said seemed nonsense to them, so they did not believe them" (Luke 24:11). Jesus appeared to the two on the road to Emmaus, who, like the women, went and told the disciples. Did they believe them? No. As the two men were explaining, Jesus appeared to them. Rather than believe, the 11 disciples "were startled and terrified, thinking they were seeing a ghost" (Luke 24:37). Jesus asked them why they were doubting, and "he showed them his hands and his feet" (Luke 24:40). Thus, it is really not fair to single out Thomas as the doubter. The only ones who believed were the women.

From all this, it would seem that doubts were not the exception; they were common, even the norm. It is not so much that we have doubts, but what do we do with them. We should not try to deny them or pretend they do not exist and hope they go away, but we should seek answers. Like Israel, we should struggle with God as we seek to understand him and his will for us.

FAITH AND CERTAINTY

The opposite of doubt is certainty, and if doubt is undesirable, should we seek certainty? Several considerations should at least raise warning flags. If nothing else, there is the historical fact that those who were certain have done tremendous evil due to their certainty. One only has to look at things like the Inquisition, the treatment of heretics, and Jews to see the problems caused by those who were certain. A bit of doubt, combined with humility, can be very healthy.

Returning to the definition of faith in Hebrews 11:1, "Now faith is the assurance that what we hope for will come about and the certainty that what we cannot see exists." The word translated certainty (*elenchos* - ἔλεγχος) refers to the verification and evidence of a belief. It is not itself an absolute, but something that comes in degrees. Thus it is quite common to ask questions such as "how certain are you?" Often, people qualify their degree of certainty with a percentage as in "I am 90 percent certain."

There are four questions we should consider when talking about certainty. The first is, how certain are you? While 100 percent certain would initially seem like the easy and best answer, there is a danger in being 100 percent certain. There is no room for error when you are 100 percent certain, and thus no reason to search for further evidence. This does not mean we should never be 100 percent certain. I am 100 percent certain of a large number of things, not the least of which is that I exist and that my wife loves me. The real danger is when we are 100 percent certain about something when, in fact, we are wrong; in short, of being more certain than we should be. Such certainty happens when we do not recognize, or just ignore, what should be legitimate doubt.

Legitimate doubt is much easier to see when you are holding a minority position. It becomes much harder to be 100 percent certain when those around you are expressing differing views. The real danger is when you are in the majority, particularly when the majority censors opposing points of view. Opposing points of view keep us honest with ourselves. Still, being in the minority and able to see the pros and cons of a given view is not, by itself, a sign that you are right. It is possible to be in the minority and still be insulated from opposing points of view. Small groups can still be so cut off from opposing views that they develop a false sense of certainty. A case in point is the 39 people who committed suicide because they thought they would be picked up by a spaceship following the Hale-Bott comet. They were certain, certain enough to commit suicide, but they should not have been.

Another example would be people caught up in big conspiracy theories. Rather than determining the conclusion based on the evidence, the conclusion becomes sacrosanct. The evidence is shaped to support it. Conflicting evidence is often ignored, with claims those behind the conspiracy planted it. Therefore, the conflicting evidence is transformed into planted evidence and thus even further proof of the conspiracy. As a result, those who hold such beliefs can be certain because they are safely behind a wall of illogic that protects them from ever being challenged.

The second question is, what is the object of your faith, what is it you are certain about? One might answer Jesus or Christianity, but these are very broad terms, and people define them in a lot of different ways. One could say the teachings of the Bible about Jesus or Christianity. Still, there are various views, even among Christians. Is it the theology or the relationship in which you have faith? I am certain in my faith in Jesus, but I am also certain that I do not know everything. These are important distinctions to make. I believe the Bible is inerrant, that it is without error in what its authors intended to say. I also believe that my understanding of what the Bible teaches is not inerrant. This is why I believe that prayer and study are so important. If I were 100 percent certain of what I believed, there would be no longer any need to study.

Once you are clear on what you are certain about, you come to the third question, why are you certain? I have more faith and am more certain in my Christian beliefs than when I first became a Christian. There are two main reasons for this; the first is what might be called classical evidence. Being a Christian apologist has definitely helped here. As I have read the critics of Christianity, looked at the evidence they put forth, and even been part of the debate in a small way, I have seen their arguments' flaws and errors. Also, the evidence for my views has only grown stronger over the years. But it is more than just the evidence commonly found in apologetics books, which is the second reason; it is the evidence from my own life.

Over the last 40 years of my Christian walk, as I have attempted to live the teachings of Christ, they have strengthened my faith. This is not to say that everything has been easy. In fact, one of the most difficult times occurred shortly after my wife and I discovered that for several months we had both separately been praying for a deeper understanding of faith in our individual prayers. Once we discovered this, we began praying together for faith. Some very difficult years followed.

There is a saying among Christians that you should not pray for patience because God will give you something about which to be patient. Patience is a tough lesson to learn, particularly in today's instant gratification culture, where issues are resolved by the end of the movie or show. Today's culture wants everything now. It is tough to learn to wait.

I believe the lesson of faith is even harder. Patience requires you to wait. Faith frequently requires you to both wait and act. You must act now, trusting God for the results in the future. Faith is easy when everything is going as you want. It becomes much tougher when things are difficult. It is the hard times that teach us the best lessons. This is the message that James has at the beginning of his letter,

> Consider it pure joy, my brothers, when you are involved in various trials, because you know that the testing of your faith produces endurance. But you must let endurance have its full effect, so that you may be mature and complete, lacking nothing. (James 1:2-4)

As you live a life of faith, seeking God's guidance, your faith will grow. There are several things I look back on that were difficult, things like going through Basic Training or teaching at Juvenile Hall, but now I am glad I did. While filling out the application to become a substitute teacher, there was a place to check off where you were willing to teach: regular school; schools for those with disabilities; community school, where students kicked out of regular school went; and finally, Juvenile Hall. I checked off all except Juvenile Hall; that was something I did not want to do.

God had other plans. I was not teaching as often as I needed. So when asked if I would re-consider Juvenile Hall, I said yes. Before long, the one place I did not want to go was where I went most often, including a week teaching in one of the two cell blocks reserved for those in for capital crimes. But God was not done yet. Because of a bureaucratic dispute over a position, I spent 18 months as a substitute teaching in the same classroom at the Youth Justice Center (YJC), a part of Juvenile Hall. The students at YJC were on probation but considered too much of a problem even for Community School. It was, in a very real sense, the last chance for an education.

It was very difficult. I was teaching Social Studies, but my primary goal was to teach them to function in a classroom. I must have done something right, for as a substitute, I was there on a day to day basis, and each day was a struggle. There certainly were times I wanted to quit. But I didn't. As James said, "But you must let endurance have its full effect" (James 1:4). I did learn a lot, and I think it made me a better person. Now, I look back on it, and I am glad I did it, even if I would not want to do it again.

It also resulted in one of those interesting "coincidences" that I do not think was actually a coincidence. After 18 months, they finally resolved the issue that had required a substitute. I left YJC and went back into the normal pool of substitutes. I was not too concerned as I was finishing up my MBA and was preparing for a job search. I would have been leaving YJC soon in any event. Yet, for a month, I was not called to substitute. When I finally called in to see why I had not been given any classes, it seems those who assign the substitutes each day did not know I was back in the pool. With that resolved, I got my first call within a few days. It turned out to be my last job as a substitute: Juvenile Hall again.

During my lunch break, I decided to wander over to YJC to see how things were going. I discovered they were doing a gradu-ation ceremony/party of sorts. It was wonderful to see so many of the students I had worked with for so long graduating. Some were returning to regular High School. Some were graduating from High School, and some were even heading off to the local Community College.

While I was standing there thanking God and thinking I had been so blessed to have just happened to have been teaching at Juvenile Hall that day, I received a call. It seems I was graduating as well, as the call was for a job. I had reached out to a former employer for a recommendation. Rather than a recommendation, he wanted to hire me. Was all this just a coincidence? Possibly, but I really don't think so, and it is just one of the many reasons my faith is stronger today.

Finally, there is the fourth question: for whom are you certain? This question is critical if we are to avoid the problems that have happened historically with certainty. The primary message of the Bible is for us as individuals. It is a message of reconciliation with God. He does not reconcile groups; he reconciles individuals, one at a time. Even when the reconciliation occurs as part of a large group, such as at a revival meeting or a Billy Graham Crusade, where hundreds of people reconcile with God, each person's salva-tion is very personal. It is an individual act.

While the Bible does teach about the church, the focus re-mains on the individual. The focus is on you and what you should be doing. Jesus warns us about being overly concerned about what others are doing, and this is the main idea behind his statement in Matthew 7,

> "Stop judging, so that you won't be judged, ₂because the way that you judge others will be the way that you will be judged, and you will be evaluated by the standard with which you evaluate others. ₃"Why do you see the speck in your brother's eye but fail to notice the beam in your own eye? ₄Or how can you say to your brother, 'Let me take the speck out of your eye,' when the beam is in your own eye? ₅You hypocrite! First remove the beam from your own eye, and then you will see clearly enough to remove the speck from your brother's eye." (Matthew 7:1-5)

A quick way to end up in trouble is to see the Bible as mainly discussing what others should be doing. Sadly, this has been demonstrated far too often in history.

Given that a key aspect of faith is that it leads to action, i.e., it leads one to act on their beliefs, we should be certain enough in our beliefs to act. We should be certain enough to pray. We should be certain enough to read and study the Bible and incorporate what we learn into how we live. Still, we should have enough doubt to realize that we do not know everything. We should temper our knowledge with wisdom and humility. We should always be cautious when we transfer our certainty to others. As Jesus put it, "remove the beam from your own eye, and then you will see clearly enough to remove the speck from your brother's eye."

CHAPTER 3

REASON
AND THE BIBLE

"Come let us reason together," says the Lord (Isaiah 1:18)

The true Jesus of Christianity made it clear that we walk by faith. He often lectured His followers about being confounded and fixated upon their physical senses. Faith is so strong an attribute that we are told even a grain of it can move mountains. Faith is the cake; everything else is just the icing. – George

As is often the case, when I pointed to evidence that conflicted with what he believed, George responded by diminishing the importance of evidence. As we saw in the last chapter, faith is, as George claimed, central to Christianity. Was he correct that everything else is just icing on the cake? Is evidence important if, and only if, it agrees with your faith? If you have evidence to support your beliefs, then great, it is like icing on a cake. If the evidence is against your beliefs, then is it really no big deal? Is it the cake that matters?

What about George's other point? Is this an either-or situation where one must choose between faith and evidence? Is there something unspiritual about reason and evidence? Or worse, did "the true Jesus of Christianity" teach us to stop being so concerned with the evidence? What is the role of evidence in the Bible? While it is clear that faith is central to Christianity, the Bible does not teach that faith should be blind. It teaches the opposite.

Both Judaism and Christianity are more than just interesting ideas that one either accepts or rejects; they are religions claiming miraculous historical events as a foundation. For Judaism, the miraculous event is the Exodus, God's leading the Jewish people out of the bondage of slavery in Egypt and into freedom. Throughout, the Hebrew Scriptures refers to God, not simply as a God in whom we should have faith, but as in Psalm 81:10, "I am the LORD your God, who brought you out of the land of Egypt." For Christianity, the central event is the resurrection, freedom from the bondage of sin. In fact, the resurrection is so central to the Christian faith that the apostle Paul said, "if the Messiah has not been raised, your faith is worthless" (1 Corinthians 15:17).

For most Jews and Christians, these are not just symbolic pictures that teach some deeper spiritual truth. These are actual historical events, events that demonstrate the truthfulness of their belief. These are the key pieces of evidence upon which they base their faith. Thus, at their core, both Judaism and Christianity are religions solidly grounded in evidence. Why should a Jew have faith in God? Because He was the one that led the Jews out of slavery and into freedom. Why should a Christian have faith in God? Because Jesus died for our sins and rose from the dead, allowing us to be set free from sin. Both faiths, at their core, are grounded in evidence and reason.

REASON IN THE OLD TESTAMENT

From the very beginnings of the Jewish religion, reason and faith have gone hand in hand. God spoke to the early Jews through prophets, and when a prophet spoke in the name of the Lord, it was the same as if God had spoken directly.

> Then the LORD told me: 'What they have suggested is good. I will raise up a prophet like you from among their relatives, and I will place my words in his mouth so that he may expound everything that I have commanded to them. But if someone will not listen to those words that the prophet speaks

in my name, I will hold him accountable. (Deuteronomy 18:17-19)

God would send prophets to speak for him, and the people would be held accountable for heeding or failing to heed what the prophets said. Of course, there was a problem with this. Anyone could claim to be a prophet, and as it turned out, many made just such claims. Moses not only told them to listen to the prophets, but he also told them to beware of the false prophets that were sure to come.

> Even then, if the prophet speaks presumptuously in my name, which I didn't authorize him to speak, or if he speaks in the name of other gods, that prophet must die.' (Deuteronomy 18:20)

How does one tell the difference between a true prophet and a false prophet? How were the Israelites to tell who really was a prophet whose messages they needed to trust and follow from the messages that were not from God and they could ignore? In this area, again, God did not expect blind faith but instead gave the Israelites a means of testing those who claimed to be prophets. Moses set out two of these tests in his final speech to the Israelites recorded in the book of Deuteronomy,

> Now you may ask yourselves, 'How will we be able to discern that the LORD has not spoken?' Whenever a prophet speaks in the name of the LORD, and the oracle does not come about or the word is not fulfilled, then the LORD has not spoken it. The prophet will have spoken presumptuously, so you need not fear him. (Deuteronomy 18:21,22)

God has warned the Jews to beware of those who would claim to be from Him but who were actually false prophets. To tell the difference between a prophet sent by God and a false prophet, God at times included in his messages things which no human could know: knowledge concerning the future. If a prophet claimed to speak for God predicting the future, and what they say does not occur, they are a false prophet. Ignore them.

Notice that this test is a negative one. It can show that a person is a false prophet. Still, simply a correct prediction of the future by itself is not enough to prove that a person is a prophet. After all, given enough predictions, some are bound to come true, and any false prophet worth his salt would only highlight the ones that worked out. Deuteronomy 13:1-3 makes this clear and gives another test to consider,

> A prophet or a diviner of dreams may arise among you, give you an omen or a miracle that takes place, and then he may tell you, 'Let's follow other gods (whom you have not known) and let's serve them.' Even though the sign or portent comes to pass, you must not listen to the words of that prophet or that diviner of dreams. For the LORD your God is testing you, to make known whether or not you'll continue to love the LORD your God with all your heart and soul.

In short, the teaching of a true prophet sent by God must not lead people to worship a god that is different from the God of the Exodus that Moses had taught the Jews to follow. This test is more theological and is just the logical result of God's descriptions found in the Bible. God knows everything (Psalm 147:4), never changes (Malachi 3:6), and does not lie (1 Samuel 15:29). There is no possibility of him saying anything that would conflict with what he had said before. As such, if a person claims to speak for God, teaching something conflicting with what God has said in the past, they are a false prophet.

A few places in the Bible predict distant future events, and the end time predictions remain to occur. Still, most of the predictions of the future were of events that would happen quickly to give validity to the prophet's other statements. For the longer-term predictions that appear, many of those were conditional, based on people's behavior. The Prophets did not restrict themselves to merely predicting the future. In fact, very little of the Bible concerns predictions of the future. A lot of the Bible is narrative describing what happened. Most of the prophets were very critical of what they saw the people around them doing. Their messages were calls to better behavior. That the Hebrew scripture is so critical of the Jews instead of putting them in the best light possible is evidence for its reliability. If someone was going to make up something about themselves, wouldn't it say how wonderful they were?

While teaching, the prophets were not restricted to repeating past teachings. The Bible speaks to particular groups of people living at particular times. It spoke to them where they were. As the people began to learn these teachings, the subsequent revelation could expand on the previous revelation providing new details not previously discussed but in harmony with the earlier teachings. New revelation can supplement and expand on early revelation, but it cannot contradict with earlier revelation.

Whether new revelation expands or contradicts the previous revelation is one of the major issues between Christians and Jews. Jews, applying this test, claim that the Christian view of God as Father, Son, and Holy Spirit is a change that contradicts the Jewish view that there is only one God. On the other hand, Christians see the Christian view of God, which historically has come to be called the Trinity[13], as a more complete revelation of God. Since the Trinity holds there is only one God, it agrees with the Jewish teaching of monotheism.

The third test for a prophet is also a logical deduction from the biblical statements about God. Jeremiah 23:9-40 is a description of false prophets and some of the ways one can identify them. In addition to tests already given, Jeremiah includes,

> They strengthen the hands of those who do evil,
>   so that no one repents of his evil.
> They keep on saying to those who despise me,
>   'The Lord has said, "You will have peace."'

---

13   These are general statements, not absolute. For a more complete discussion of the theology see Elgin L Hushbeck, Jr, *Christianity: The Basics*, (Gonzales, FL: Energion, 2017)

To all who stubbornly follow their own desires they say,
   'Disaster won't come upon you.' (Jeremiah 23:14, 17)

One of the things the Bible teaches about God is that he is righteous (Psalm 33:4-5) and opposes those who rebel against Him (Psalm 5:4). Any prophet who claims to speak in the name of the Lord and supports those who do evil cannot be truly be speaking for God.

The Jewish religion was grounded in the evidence of the Exodus. The words of prophets guided the Jews. These prophets were not to be accepted by faith but tested based on a rational evaluation of the evidence. Reason and evidence played a central role in the very origin of the Hebrew Scriptures. Since God never changes, we can expect the same to be true of the New Testament.

REASON IN THE NEW TESTAMENT

Some claim that while evidence and reason played a role in the Jewish religion, that changed with Christianity. Now we live by faith. Yet when it comes to faith and reason, the choice is not either/or. Christianity does place a strong emphasis on faith. Yet, as we saw in the last chapter, the author of Hebrews demonstrates this is nothing new as faith has always been an integral part of God's plan. Just as faith played an important role in the Old Testament, reason plays an important role in the New.

While on his missionary journeys, when Paul preached about Jesus, he did not ask people simply to have blind faith in what he said. Instead, he expected people to question his claims and challenged people to check them out. For example, some of the new Christians in the Greek city of Corinth, undoubtedly influenced by Greek philosophy that downplayed the importance of the material world, questioned the need to believe that Christ rose physically from the dead. Paul did not respond with demands that they simply have faith. Instead, he replied in 1 Corinthians 15 with a well-reasoned defense of the physical resurrection based on the evidence.

After describing the centrality of the resurrection in the Gospel message (15:1-4), Paul proceeds to list those who saw the risen Lord (15:5-11) and thus who served as evidence that the resurrection actually occurred. Of particular note is his statement in verse 6 that "…he was seen by more than 500 brothers at one time, most of whom are still alive, though some have died." Paul is not only pointing out that Jesus appeared to 500 people, but he goes on to make it clear that most of these people were still living at the time he wrote. Pointing out that most were still alive has little significance except to say they could support Paul's claims. Those who did not believe Paul could check out what he said. They could go and speak to those who witnessed it. Paul was not only giving evidence to support the Resurrection; he was challenging those in Corinth to check it out for themselves.

After establishing the Resurrection was a historical event witnessed by many people, Paul then proceeds to discuss the ramifications of rejecting the resurrection. To do this, he uses a series of logical "if then" arguments.

> If there is no resurrection of the dead, then the Messiah has not been raised, and if the Messiah has not been raised, then our message means nothing and your faith means nothing. In addition, we are found to be false witnesses about God because we testified on God's behalf that he raised the Messiah—whom he did not raise if in fact it is true that the dead are not raised. For if the dead are not raised, then the Messiah has not been raised, and if the Messiah has not been raised, your faith is worthless and you are still imprisoned by your sins. Yes, even those who have died believing in the Messiah are lost. If we have set our hopes on the Messiah in this life only, we deserve more pity than any other people. (1 Corinthians 15:13-19)

Paul did not restrict his use of reason and evidence simply to those within the Church who already had faith. In Acts 17, Luke records Paul's visit to Athens, which occurred around A.D. 50. There, Paul "began holding discussions in the synagogue with the

Jews and other worshipers, as well as every day in the public square with anyone who happened to be there." (Acts 17:17).

The word translated as "discussions" is the Greek word *dielegeto* (διελέγετο), from where we get the English word dialogue. It means to discuss rationally, usually with the goal of teaching. For example, Greek philosophers used it to describe their question-and-answer method of teaching. This term is a common one used to describe Paul's style of speaking.[14]

Paul's teachings in the marketplace of Athens attracted the attention of some Epicurean and Stoic philosophers. While their exact motives in doing so are unclear, they brought Paul before the Areopagus to present his "new teachings" (Acts 17:18-19). The Areopagus consisted of those city officials who had finished their terms without misconduct. Since Athens had come under Roman rule, the Areopagus had lost much of the authority. However, when Paul appeared before this body, it retained authority over religion, morality, and education. Paul's speech before the Areopagus gives us a good example of how he presented the Gospel. He used evidence and reason.

Paul begins by establishing common ground upon which to build his case by pointing to their belief in "an unknown god" (Acts 17:22-23). He then builds his case, beginning with the creation of the world. From creation, he drew conclusions about the true God.

> The God who made the world and everything in it is the Lord of heaven and earth. He doesn't live in shrines made by human hands, and he isn't served by people as if he needed anything. He himself gives everyone life, breath, and every-thing else. (Acts 17:24-25)

Paul then moves on to a discussion of man's relationship with God. He uses quotations from Epimenides and Aratus, two Greek poets with whom those in the Areopagus would have been familiar as evidence to support his case. Finally, Paul concludes by pointing out that,

---

14   Also see Acts 17:2; 18:4, 19; 19:8; 20:7, 9; 24:12, 25

Though God has overlooked those times of ignorance, he now commands everyone everywhere to repent, because he has set a day when he is going to judge the world with justice through a man whom he has appointed. He has given proof of this to everyone by raising him from the dead." (Acts 17:30-31)

While some sneered at the "proof" that God had provided, others did not. One of those who accepted Paul's rational argument was Dionysius, who was later said to have become the first Bishop of Athens.[15] Thus to Paul, the Gospel and the Resurrection were not things to be accepted blindly. He did not call upon people to just have faith but supported them with reason and evidence. These were things that could stand up to testing.

As a result, Paul challenged people to test what he said. He did not criticize them for lacking faith when they did but instead praised them. At his arrival in the Greek city of Berea, as was his custom, Paul went to the Jewish synagogue. Hearing the Gospel message, the Jews in this city did not blindly put their faith in what Paul said. Instead, "These people were more receptive than those in Thessalonica. They were very willing to receive the message, and every day they carefully examined the Scriptures to see if those things were so." (Acts 17:11) The word translated as "more receptive" in this passage has a positive overtone, and many translations translate it as "noble."

This is thoroughly in line with the rest of the New Testament teachings. Rather than follow blindly, we instead are told to "test everything. Hold on to what is good." (1 Thessalonians 5:21) The Apostle John wrote, "Dear friends, stop believing every spirit. Instead, test the spirits to see whether they are from God, because many false prophets have gone out into the world." (1 John 4:1) As we saw in the last chapter, Abraham, when confronted with what he thought was a conflict in what God had told him, used reason to reconcile the conflict (Hebrews 11:19).

---

15   Robert M. Grant, *Greek Apologists of the Second Century* (Philadelphia: The Westminster Press, 1988) p. 106

REASON AND JESUS CHRIST

Returning to the question that began this chapter, did "the true Jesus of Christianity" teach that we should stop being so concerned with the evidence? Of course, one could argue it is one thing to test prophets, apostles, or even "spirits," but to test Jesus Christ is different altogether. However, this was not Jesus' attitude.

In his Gospel, John records that Jesus was in Jerusalem for the Feast of Dedication (Hanukkah), which took place a few months before he was crucified. By this time, Jesus had been teaching for about three years and encountered the Jewish Leader several times. He had done many miracles and had gathered quite a following. Several months before, during the Feast of Tabernacles, there had been a lot of discussion among the crowd as to who Jesus really was (John 7:11-13). Some thought he was a prophet, some the Christ. Others were not so sure, while others were sure he was not (John 7:40-44).

One day, a group gathered around him at the temple. They wanted to settle these questions about his identity once and for all. They asked him, "How long are you going to keep us in suspense? If you're the Messiah, tell us so plainly" (John 10:24). Jesus began his reply by saying, "I have told you, but you don't believe it. The actions that I do in my Father's name testify on my behalf" (John 10:25).

In answering their question, Jesus did not appeal to a statement of faith, but to the evidence, to the things that he did, demonstrating who he truly was. He did not expect them to simply believe his claims. In fact, in John 5:31, Jesus said: "If I testify on my own behalf, my testimony is not trustworthy." Jesus was not saying he was untrustworthy, but rather that the true Messiah would not come without supporting evidence. Jesus then proceeded to cite the testimony of John the Baptist (John 5:33-35), the works of the father he has done (e.g., miracles) (5:36), and the statements in the Scriptures about him (5:37-40). All this was evidence of who he was.

In John 10, after pointing to the evidence that should have told them who he was, Jesus answers their question about his identity with a claim to be God (John 10:30). At this point, the Jews accuse him of blasphemy and "picked up stones to stone him to death" (John 10:31). Jesus responded to the charge of blasphemy, again not with an appeal to faith, but rather a rational argument refuting their claim that he had blasphemed.

> Is it not written in your Law, 'I said, "You are gods"'? If he called those to whom a message from God came 'gods' (and the Scripture cannot be disregarded), how can you say to the one whom the Father has consecrated and sent into the world, 'You're blaspheming,' because I said, 'I'm the Son of God'? (John 10:34-36)

In his response, Jesus uses a quotation from Psalm 82:6 as his premise. There are several theories as to exactly who is called gods in this Psalm[16]. Fortunately, that does not concern us here. It does not affect either the fact that this is a logical argument or its conclusion. The premise's key point is that the God of Israel referred to something other than himself as "gods" in Psalm 82:6.

Jesus' argument is simply a modified if-then type of argument. He states his conclusion in the form of a rhetorical question pointing out that he has far more right to be called God than those in Psalm 82:6. He argues that since he has more right to be called God than those in Psalm 82:6, if it was not blasphemy for them to be called god, it cannot be blasphemy for him to be called God. Note that when the Jews accused him of blasphemy for claiming to be God, Jesus did not argue they had misunderstood him. Instead, he argues it was not blasphemous for him to make the claim. By

---

16 Some of the major suggestions are the judges of Israel, the generation who came out of Egypt, or the false gods of the nations surrounding Israel. The context of John 10 and Jesus' statement that the "Word of God came" to these "gods" would seem to support the first two options. Uses of *elohim* (the word translated god in Psalm 82) in Exodus 22:8,9 and 1 Samuel 2:25 supports the belief these were judges.

doing so, Jesus confirmed their basic understanding, i.e., he had claimed to be God, was correct.

Thus as we have seen, when questioned about his identity, Jesus responded with an appeal to the evidence and logical arguments, i.e., when charged with blaspheme, He defended himself with reason. But Jesus did not stop there and went on to say:

> If I'm not doing my Father's actions, don't believe me. But if I'm doing them, even though you don't believe me, believe the actions, so that you may know and understand that the Father is in me and I am in the Father." (John 10:36-38)

A more direct statement of the importance of evidence is hard to imagine. Jesus could have said that those questioning Him should just have faith, yet he does the opposite. He tells them they should not believe him unless he is "doing my Father's actions," i.e., miracles from the father. In short, do not believe Jesus unless he has the evidence to back up his claims. Jesus then says if they don't believe him, they should at least believe the evidence that demonstrates who he is.

Thus, evidence is far from being "just the icing" on the cake; nice if you have it, but not needed. On the contrary, we have seen that reason and evidence play a significant role in both Judaism and Christianity. Evidence and reason alone cannot save. They can, at best, lead only to belief. Salvation requires faith, a trust in our beliefs that leads to action. Evidence and reason still serve an important role, for they help us know whether our faith is placed correctly. They can provide a foundation for our beliefs, helping us avoid error, but it is still faith, our beliefs put into action, that saves.

Reason and evidence, when correctly applied, give us tools in determining what is true and what is an error. The tools of reason and evidence that supports truth support the one who said: "I am the way and the truth and the life." So in the next section, we will look at some of these "tools" and how they can be used to determine the truth and eliminate errors.

Part II
Reason &
Thinking

CHAPTER 4

CRITICAL
THINKING

"Put forward your case!" says the Lord.
    "Submit your arguments!" says Jacob's King. (Isaiah 41:21)

What is really sad about your case is that you think you actually make valid points about Greek, history, logic, the Bible, etc. It is all a canned and closed system you have fashioned… But I have to give it to you; you have the neatest little system. – John

Though meant as an attack, I agreed with John. Reason and logic are, in many respects, "a canned and closed system." Most systems are. The difference is that reason and logic form a generic system designed not to support a preconceived conclusion but instead to discover truth and eliminate error. They not only apply to my discussion with John but to all realms, where identifying the truth and removing mistakes are important.

Critical thinking is just a system of rules and guidelines, helping us evaluate and judge the evidence correctly to reach valid conclusions. Drawing conclusions based on evidence is easy; we do it all the time. The trick is to draw the correct conclusions and to reject any that are invalid. In the next few chapters, we will look at some of the ways we can go wrong in our thinking. First, let us look at what defines critical thinking.

In Matthew Chapter 12, Jesus casts out the demons possessing a man. Because he could control the demons to the point of commanding them to leave the man, the Pharisees concluded that

Jesus' power came from Beelzebub, the prince of demons. Jesus, not too surprisingly, said they were in error. What makes the Pharisees' conclusion wrong and Jesus' correct? Is it merely a matter of whom you choose to believe? Not at all. One only has to examine the arguments on both sides to see that the claim of the Pharisees was flawed as Jesus refutes it with reasoning, demonstrating the truthfulness of his position.

The Pharisees did not dispute that Jesus had the power to perform this miracle; after all, they had seen the evidence right in front of them. Instead, they concluded his power came from Beelzebub. To demonstrate the flaw in their reasoning, Jesus asked them,

> Every kingdom divided against itself is destroyed, and every city or household divided against itself will not stand. So if Satan drives out Satan, he is divided against himself. How, then, can his kingdom stand? (Matthew 25:26-26)

There is an unstated premise here. It is a premise the Pharisees accepted as a given and did not need stating, i.e., that Satan wanted to advance his kingdom. Granted, this is a premise that some today would question, but that was not the case with the Pharisees to whom Jesus was talking. So there was no need for Jesus to include this premise in his argument. If the Pharisees were correct, and Jesus was acting by the power of Satan, Satan was working against his own goals, thereby revealing a tremendous contradiction in the Pharisee's argument. It was flawed thinking. It is not just a matter of whom you choose to believe, but who has the better case.

WHAT IS AN ARGUMENT?

Rational arguments come in a variety of forms, but all have the same essential components. Arguments start with information that is known, or at least believed, from which information that is not known can be determined. The information that is known is referred to as a *premise*. The information that is obtained is called the *conclusion*.

Often, this order is reversed in discussions or debates, and the conclusion is given first and then defended. It is awkward to think in terms of starting with the *conclusion*. So when this happens, the statement being supported is often called a *claim;* the known information that backs it up is called a *warrant, justification,* or just *reason.* A simple form of an argument would be either:

Premise #1	All humans are mortal.
Premise #2	Abraham was human.
Conclusion	Abraham was mortal.

Or

Claim	Abraham was mortal.
Reason #1	Abraham was human.
Reason #2	All humans are mortal.

Whatever you call them, premises, warrants, justifications, and reasons are the building blocks of arguments. These must be considered true by all sides for an argument to have any chance at convincing. If there is any question about a premise, it becomes the focus of discussion until all sides accept it. Only then can the argument proceed.

There is an exception to this rule. It occurs when a premise is only accepted provisionally so the argument can proceed. This is often an excellent way to test out an argument or explain how someone could reach a particular conclusion without spending a lot of time on what would otherwise be a contentious premise. Its occurrence is usually pretty clear as the premise will be introduced with phrases such as "if for argument's sake we accept…"

VALID VERSUS INVALID ARGUMENTS

The conclusion in the argument above is correct. But we can change this if we modify it just slightly as follows,

Premise #1	All Egyptians are human.
Premise #2	Abraham was human.
Conclusion	Abraham was an Egyptian.

While the change is only slight, the argument is now logically flawed, and assuming we are referring to the biblical Abraham, clearly untrue. Why does this argument fail while the previous one works? Premise #2 of both arguments state that Abraham was human. For this to be true, all aspects of being human must apply to Abraham. As such, any sentence that applies to all humans also applies to Abraham. For sentences that describe all humans, you can replace the words 'all human' with 'Abraham,' and it will still be correct.

Doing this replacement with the first argument gives you the conclusion "Abraham is mortal," and therefore, the conclusion is valid. No such substitution is possible in the second argument. While the second premise says, "Abraham was human," the first premise does not speak of all humans, but all Egyptians. Thus, there is no direct connection between these two premises. The conclusion that "Abraham was an Egyptian" is not a reasonable one.

If all this discussion of replacing parts of one premise with parts from another to get a conclusion sounds a bit like solving algebraic equations, you are not too far off. In Formal Logic, philosophers convert the structures of various arguments into symbols. Then proofs are developed to show whether particular structures lead to certain conclusions. Those structures that lead to dependable conclusions are called valid, and those that do not are called invalid.

SOUND VERSUS UNSOUND ARGUMENTS

The argument is considered sound when both the premises are true and the structure is valid. Sound arguments have conclusions that must be accepted. A problem with either the premises or the structure of an argument means it is unsound and cannot be trusted. It is important to note that there is a difference between valid/invalid arguments and sound/unsound arguments. While it is easy to confuse these concepts, they are not quite the same. Valid/invalid refers only to the argument's structure, not whether the conclusion should be accepted. A valid argument can still have a false conclusion. For example, the following argument is a valid one and yet has a false conclusion:

> All dogs are reptiles.
> Poodles are dogs.
> Therefore, poodles are reptiles.

While logically valid, this is not a sound argument. It is valid because it is correctly structured. It is unsound because the first premise (All dogs are reptiles) is false. A correctly structured argument is still only as good as the premises upon which it is based. This is why there must be agreement on the premises before an argument can proceed.

Just as the conclusion of a valid argument can be false, the conclusion of an invalid argument can still be true.

> All cows are mammals.
> Poodles are dogs.
> Therefore, Poodles are mammals.

In this nonsensical argument, both of the premises are true, as is the conclusion. Still, it is an invalid argument because the conclusion does not logically follow from the premises. While this may seem confusing, the key is, while we happen to know from other means that this conclusion is true, we cannot determine this from the argument itself.

This brings up a very important point; a bad argument for something is not the same as an argument against something. An unsound argument gives you no information one way or the other, except that the argument was unsound. Rejecting something based on an unsound argument is just as faulty as accepting it. Thus, the argument above is not a reason to reject that poodles are mammals; it just cannot be used to show that they are.

This concept will be important to remember in the coming chapters, as I give many examples of erroneous thinking. Errors in thinking are very common. I may use some from positions you accept. While some examples are from positions I disagree with, others are from positions I hold, even if I reject the particular argument used for the example. An error in an argument only shows the argument cannot be trusted, not that the position itself is wrong.

One thing about invalid arguments is that if the conclusion is true, they can often be fixed with minor modifications. In this example, the argument can be made valid by simply changing the first premise to "All dogs are mammals."

PARADIGMS

A more difficult problem with premises has to do with paradigms. A paradigm is simply the conceptual framework in which we understand and evaluate facts; in short, it is the way we look at the world. An example of a paradigm in action is the classic question; is the glass half empty or half full? In evaluating evidence, we must evaluate it in relation to something; this will be what we already believe. This is one of the major reasons two people can look at the same evidence and reach different conclusions.

The really difficult thing about paradigms is that they are often so taken for granted that it is difficult to evaluate other positions. Paradigms are taken for granted to such an extent that they are just assumed to be true, normally without even realizing we are accepting them.

I was once talking with an atheist whose view of reality, his paradigm, left no place for anything other than the natural world. I cited evidence for the existence of the supernatural, and he ignored it.[17] When I pointed out that he was not addressing the arguments I was making, he replied,

> "Have you ever considered that whatever it is that you think are points that have real probative value are actually so lacking in probative value that it is only YOU that sees them as points?"

---

17   Elgin L Hushbeck, Jr, *Christianity and Secularism*, pp. 47-66

His view did not change even when I pointed out that it was not just me. These arguments are taken seriously by philosophers and others. It did not matter. Even the possibility that the supernatural could exist was so far removed from his view of reality that he could not seriously consider any argument supporting it. He literally could not comprehend them and, as such, never did give any specific reason for rejecting them.

While by no means limited to religion, the concept of paradigms helps explain why many discussions can be difficult. For example, a Christian and a Buddhist approach reality from radically different perspectives. The Christian's goal is personal salvation, the salvation of the self; the Buddhist's goal is the realization that the self does not exist, the annihilation of the self. Because of these different views of reality, Buddhists and Christians will evaluate the evidence differently. Often, the hardest part of such discussions is finding common premises upon which both sides can agree and base an argument.

COMMON GROUND

Central to any argument are the premises, as these are the foundation. There must be agreement on the validity of the premises for an argument to be effective. For example, I could easily construct a valid argument demonstrating that God created humans as follows:

> God created the entire universe.
> Humans are part of the universe.
> Therefore, God created humans.

The above argument is logically valid, and I believe both premises to be true. Therefore it is sound, and I accept the conclusion as true. Still, I would never use this argument with an atheist. An atheist will undoubtedly reject the first premise and will not find this argument very convincing. When disagreements such as this occur, the proper way to proceed is to begin justifying the premises that are in dispute – in this case, the premise that "God created the entire universe."

This process of working backward through arguments looking for premises upon which both sides can agree is searching for common ground. Otherwise, neither side's arguments will seem very convincing to the other. The failure to do this important step is why many arguments go around and around without ever getting anywhere. For example, atheists will never find arguments that God created the universe very convincing since they do not believe in God. Before you can determine whether God created the universe, you must first establish that God exists!

FOUNDATIONS

If they are the foundation of all arguments, from where do premises come? Normally these are known facts or at least things accepted by all sides. Often they are themselves the conclusions of other arguments. In questioning a premise, we must go back to the arguments that supported it until we reach a set of premises accepted by both sides. In other words, we must establish a solid foundation upon which to build our arguments.

How far back can this search go? Is it a never-ending series of conclusions based on even earlier premises? Is it possible that one would never reach common ground? While theoretically possible, I have never encountered anyone with whom I could not find at least some common ground upon which to base a discussion, given enough time.

After all, we are not beings who gain all our knowledge through logical and rational analysis. Much of what we know and believe we have just acquired, picking up bits and pieces as we live our lives. We gain knowledge through experiences and from others. The knowledge from others can come from parents, friends, teachers, books, movies, podcasts, and any number of sources. Thus the more similar the backgrounds, the easier it will be to find common ground.

This method of learning is one of the reasons discussions are so important. While some of the things we "know" were accepted critically, most were not. We all inherit a whole range of beliefs from the culture we grow up in, without really understanding why we believe them or from where they came. At times these are so taken for granted we do not realize that others do not accept them. We do not realize that these beliefs are actually the conclusions of arguments we never saw.

For example, having been influenced for 2000 years by the Bible, Western Civilization has a view of human life as import-ant in a way that would have been completely foreign in ancient Greece and Rome. Today it is a given. If you were to travel in time to ancient Rome and start talking about the importance of human rights, nobody would have the faintest idea of what you were talking about. If someone from ancient Rome were to travel our time, they would be completely perplexed by all discussion of conflicting competing rights.

It is through discussion that we can bring these underlying beliefs into the light. We can test them and evaluate the pros and cons for them. In doing so, we can transform them from hidden assumptions to reasoned conclusions. As a result, we gain not only a better understanding of what we believe but also why.

PREMISE ZERO

Reasoning must have some starting place, a premise zero if you like. This starting place is very important. After all, if you make a false assumption with premise zero, then your whole view of reality would be suspect. Premise zero divides Evidential and Presuppositional Apologetics. Presuppositional apologetics holds that everything must start with God. Therefore, it follows logically that Christian apologetics must start with God. This starting point normally works well when dealing with those who are already the-ists. However, this results in the fallacy of circular reasoning when dealing with atheists.

But if we do not start with God, where do we start? What is a premise zero that nearly all will agree is true? I believe the best candidate for premise zero is self-existence – Descartes' "Cogito, ergo sum," Latin for I think; therefore, I am. Modern philosophers have questioned Descartes's conclusion. They argue he assumes something called 'I.' These philosophers claim his argument only shows that there is thinking taking place, not that there is an 'I' thinking. Still, it will serve in most real-life discussions[18].

While from a philosophical perspective, I am making great leaps from the fact that you exist, hopefully, it is not that difficult to conclude that we both exist. Not only do we exist, but we also exist in a world that we can experience and experience commonly. At least common enough to communicate about the world around us. We can gain some understanding of our world from these shared experiences. It is from these experiences that we build our view of reality. This view of reality is where logic and reason come into play.

REAL WORLD ARGUMENTS

One difficulty in analyzing logical arguments is that, except in textbooks on logic, arguments are rarely as simple and well structured as presented. The arguments given by Jesus and the Pharisees at the beginning of this chapter are good examples of logical arguments in real-world discussions. Here is Jesus' argument put in the form of premise and conclusion:

Premise #1	Every kingdom divided against itself will be ruined, and every city or household divided against itself will not stand.
Premise #2	If Satan drives out Satan, he is divided against himself.
Conclusion	How then can his kingdom stand?

---

18 Arguments that question the existence of 'I' quickly become a discussion on the nature of consciousness, and these discussions are are well beyond the scope of this book.

The first thing we see is Jesus' conclusion is not in the form of a statement but a rhetorical question. The implied answer is that his kingdom couldn't stand if Satan did this. Also, as discussed earlier, Jesus' argument used an implied premise, a premise so well understood it did not need to be stated explicitly. It could be assumed. In this case, the implied premise is that Satan seeks to build his kingdom, not tear it down.

Using implied premises is perfectly legitimate and is highly desirable. Normally when presenting an argument, you want to limit your premises to the key ones needed to demonstrate your point. For example, when trying to show a person could easily have seen an accident, you might say it occurred in the middle of the day in plain view of the person. You would not normally need to explicitly specify that there was plenty of light or that an eclipse did not block the sun. Likewise, Jesus did not need to specify that Satan wants to build his kingdom.

Of course, the danger of using an implied premise is that the person you are trying to convince may not accept the premise. Therefore, your argument will not seem complete or convincing. Fortunately, we can remedy this very easily; make the premise explicit when questioned. In the example above, if someone questions your premise that there was plenty of light, you could point out that the sun was shining brightly; there were no clouds, nor was there an eclipse that day, and the accident occurred outdoors in an open area.

The key to real-world arguments is identifying the premises and conclusions and testing them to see if the premises are true and lead to the stated conclusion. While this is not always easy, one thing that makes this task easier is that it is the person's responsibility to make the argument coherent. Ask the person to clarify it if an argument is not clear.

DEDUCTION

Rational arguments come in basically two forms, deduction and induction. A deductive argument is one in which the conclusion comes directly from the premises. Up to this point in this chapter, we have been referring mostly to deductive arguments.

Premise #1	All humans are mortal.
Premise #2	Abraham was human.
Conclusion	Abraham was mortal.

This is a deductive argument. As we saw earlier, the premises lead directly and almost mathematically to the conclusion. One of the key features of a deductive argument is that if the premises are true and the argument is logically valid, then the conclusion must also be true. Because of this feature, deductive arguments are the most powerful and the most desirable. It also means there are only two ways to challenge a deductive argument.

1) Demonstrate that one or more of the premises are false
2) Demonstrate that the argument is not logically valid

The power of deductive arguments comes at a price. All the conditions and variables must be known and accounted for in the argument for the argument to be valid. Unfortunately, in many cases, this is impractical, if not outright impossible. As such, deductive arguments are normally restricted to those arguments where we can talk in absolute terms such as "all," "every," "never," "none," or where there are clear If-Then relationships.

INDUCTION

In most of the discussions you are likely to engage in, it is impossible to state things in the absolute terms required for deductive arguments. In these cases, we use induction. Induction still reasons from what we know to make conclusions about what we do not know. The difference is that since the argument does not account for everything, the conclusions are not guaranteed to be correct as they are with deductive arguments. An example of an inductive argument would be:

Premise #1	Abraham was human, and he died.
Premise #2	Moses was human, and he died.
Premise #3	Paul was human, and he died.
Premise #4	You are human.
Conclusion	You will probably die.

Notice in this argument, the conclusion is not stated to be absolutely true, but only "probably" true. While not always directly stated as such, inductive arguments are probability arguments. They are still logically valid arguments. The strength of an inductive argument is directly related to the evidence given in the premises. For example, we can strengthen the argument above by simply adding more examples to show a link between being human and dying. Yet, no matter how many examples we give to demonstrate this link, we cannot rule out that someone may be different. We cannot rule out the possibility that some discovery might allow for immortality. As such, the conclusion that you will die remains only a probability. A very high probability, but still a probability.

While inductive arguments are not guaranteed to be correct, this does not mean that they are unreliable. For example, science is an inductive process, not a deductive one. When Newton first set forth his laws of motion, this was the result of inductive reasoning. To be deductive, Newton would have had to observe all motion throughout the entire universe and throughout all time. This, of course, would be impossible. All he could do is observe motion in a few situations and then determine his laws from these observations.

Since then, his findings have been duplicated by other scientists, along with millions of students in science classes. So much so that there is no doubt about how an apple falls to the ground. Still, despite all of this testing and confirmation, Newton's laws remain a result of induction. However small, there remains the possibility that there was some aspect or circumstances for which Newton had not accounted. A possibility that his laws were not the universal laws he believed.

As it turned out, this was the case, for as Einstein demonstrated, Newton's laws do, in fact, break down as objects approach the speed of light. Thus inductive arguments can be very strong and often are considered, for all practical purposes, conclusive. Still, there always remains, at least theoretically, some small degree of doubt.

Inductive arguments are also the arguments we encounter most often in the real world. For example, statistical studies are, by their nature, inductive. This is another reason why two people can look at the same evidence and reach different conclusions. Unlike deductive arguments, inductive arguments are not binding. However small it may be, one can always latch on to the uncertainty inherent in this form of argument and declare the argument to be inconclusive. As we will see, many do just that.

INDUCTION AND FAITH

Like the real world in general, most religious arguments are inductive arguments. The arguments for God's existence, the inspiration of the Bible, and the resurrection of Jesus are inductive. They are probability arguments. For example, I believe the evidence for God's existence is not only strong, but I consider it overwhelming. Yet, as strong as the arguments may be, they are still inductive arguments. As such, they cannot conclusively prove that God exists in the same way a deductive argument would. There remains room for doubt. The atheists and agnostics can (and do) point to this doubt and claim that there is no proof that God exists. In short, they demand a deductive argument where none is possible.

Just as there is room for doubt, there is room for faith. The evidence may point to the existence of God. Still, when we accept the conclusions to which the evidence points and begin to act on those conclusions, this is faith. When we believe that God exists and, as a result of that belief, live in a way consistent with this belief, that is faith.

CHAPTER 5

NOT SO CRITICAL
THINKING:
EVIDENCE

*I say this so that no one will mislead you with nice-sounding rhetoric.
(Colossians 2:4)*

I n the first chapter, we raised the question: if reason and evidence are so reliable in determining the truth, why is there such a diversity of opinion? While there are some problems with evidence (or the lack thereof), a large part of the problem comes simply from faulty reasoning. There are many ways these errors can be categorized. Here we will divide them into two types: uncritical thinking and logical errors. The logical errors we will deal with in Chapter 7. Uncritical thinking can be divided into problems evaluating evidence, discussed in this chapter, and problems in communication or presentation, discussed in Chapter 6.[19]

General approaches to thinking, discussions, and debates that are in and of themselves unsound and prone to error are what we call uncritical thinking. Some of these are little more than debaters tricks designed to confuse and hide the real issues. While erroneous, this does not mean they are uncommon. Others are just simple mistakes. Either way, they lead to error.

Unfortunately, as we go through them, you may be surprised at how often you have encountered some of these errors. Nor are they found simply among the uneducated. These forms of uncritical thinking are so prevalent that many consider them to be

---

19 The dividing line between these categories is admittedly somewhat
    arbitrary, and is chosen solely to make the presentation easier to follow.

just another valid way to argue. They are commonly found at all education levels, occurring on all sides of major issues currently under discussion, both Christians and Non-Christians. Observe nearly any discussion on nearly any issue, and you will probably see a few of these errors in reasoning. They are so common that you will probably find you have strayed into some of these categories yourself at one time or another. After reading through these, if you can honestly say 'I never do any of these things,' then you truly are a uniquely rational person.

ONE DIMENSIONAL ARGUMENT

"Are you from Galilee too?" (John 7:52)

One of the more common problems today is the refusal to consider things rationally, particularly religion. Religion, for many, is a subject one simply does not discuss. Religious beliefs may be rejected or accepted but not considered or discussed. The refusal to discuss is not, in and of itself, a problem. There can, and are, many valid reasons not to engage in a discussion. The real problem begins when views are advocated, yet not defended, where problems are avoided, like an ostrich sticking its head in the sand, by simply ignoring them.

This problem manifests at an individual level when someone wants to tell you all the good things about what they believe. While very willing to discuss the good, they see any discussion of the problems with their beliefs as contentious, disturbing, or disruptive. At a group level, serious consideration of problems is often avoided by simply writing off those who disagree with some pejorative label so that the criticism they raise can be ignored.

A classic example of this was the Jewish Leaders' discussion concerning Jesus recorded in John 7:45-52. Nicodemus questions the attitude of the leaders, asking, "Does our Law condemn anyone without first hearing him to find out what he is doing?" Nicodemus' question was met, not with a reasoned response, but with what was from their point of view a pejorative question, "Are you from Galilee too?" – a response geared more at stifling criticism than answering it.

A disturbing trend on the societal level has been the move to frame the discussion of controversial issues in terms of "rights." Once something gains the status of a right, there is no need for further justification; discussion is over – at least theoretically. The problem is that, what is and is not a right, is by no means clear; nor is it clear which "rights" should take precedence over other rights. As a result, you often see both sides in a discussion proclaiming conflicting rights, which the other side ignores.

Nowhere is this more apparent than in the abortion discussion. Before 1972, abortion was not the divisive and controversial issue that it is now. The subject was discussed, laws were passed and modified. These laws were not passed without controversy; still, there was nowhere near the controversy now surrounding this issue. All this changed with Roe v. Wade. Suddenly abortion was no longer a matter of when life began or how to deal with difficult cases such as rape, incest, and the mother's health. Abortion was a protected constitutional right; to continue to oppose abortion was to oppose the Constitution. Case closed. Discussion over.

The problem was opponents of abortion also pointed to a right to support their case, the right to life. After all, who could be against a right to life? Thus rather than settle the issue, the court's intervention magnified the problem. A rational discussion of this issue was not only much more difficult, but the court's ruling also precluded any hope of reaching a compromise agreement. In a very real sense, the opposing sides are no longer even discussing the same question. Instead, they are arguing about different rights.

Whether on an individual, group, or societal level, the key to the One Dimensional argument is it claims the opposition's arguments do not need any serious consideration or response. There can be only one legitimate way to look at the issue.

CHERRY PICKING

> We should be particularly wary when someone refers to
> Jesus Christ as 'the Christ...'[20]

The Cherry Picking approach is one of the most common, easiest to fall into, and the most likely to affect those like myself, whose main focus is apologetics. The Cherry Picking approach to knowledge only wants to consider the evidence supporting the position one believes.

Normally there will be some evidence on both sides of any question, at least for most discussions of any substance. The best way to deal with such situations is to consider all of the information, then pick the position which explains or comes closest to explaining all of the evidence. Those who fall into the Cherry Picking error pick and choose among all the various pieces of evidence only those things that support what they want to believe; they ignore anything that conflicts.

In its mild form, this comes out as Confirmation Bias, the tendency to give greater importance to evidence that supports what you believe than evidence that does not. You hear about a study supporting a belief you have, and it becomes an important and valuable study. You hear about a study conflicting with a belief you have and see it as questionable. Many see it as funded by a group they do not like. The key difference in these reactions is the prior belief, not the merits, or lack thereof, of the studies.

In its more extreme forms, Cherry Picking does not just select among the evidence but distorts the evidence to achieve the desired outcome. A great example of an extreme Cherry Picking approach is G. A. Riplinger's book, *New Age Bible Versions*. Riplinger tries to claim that the words "the Christ" show New Age influence when found in modern Bible translations. She then lists various passages where modern translations such as the NIV and NASB translate passages as "the Christ," where the KJV says "Christ." She con-

---

20   G. A. Riplinger, *New Age Bible Versions,* (Munroe Falls, Ohio: AV
     Publications, 1993) p. 319

cludes that these modern translations are New Age Bibles. As part of her support that "the Christ" is a New Age term, she has the following quote,

> Liberty University's Dean Norman Geisler adds:
> We should be particularly wary when someone refers to Jesus Christ as 'the Christ…'[21]

What makes this such a good example of the Cherry Picking approach to evidence instantly becomes apparent when one reads Geisler's full quote.

> We should be particularly wary when someone refers to Jesus Christ as 'the Christ Spirit' or 'the Christ Consciousness.'[22]

Geisler was not even speaking about 'the Christ' as Riplinger implies in her quote, but "the Christ Spirit" or "the Christ Consciousness." Riplinger just used the part of the sentence that supports her point and left the rest out – The Cherry Picking approach; pick what you like, leave the rest.

Another component central to the Cherry Picking approach is ignoring evidence that conflicts with a position rather than dealing with it. In the case above, while "the Christ" found in modern translations is considered evidence of a New Age Influence, KJV-Only supporters ignore all the places where the KJV refers to "the Christ." Places such as Matthew 16:16, "And Simon Peter answered and said, Thou art the Christ, the Son of the living God." Such counter-evidence goes to the heart of their claim that "the Christ" shows a New Age influence.

As for the examples Riplinger cites, they show nothing more than the translators of the modern translations made a different choice about translating these passages. To see why this is even a choice, we need to look at the meaning of the Greek word rendered as 'Christ' in the New Testament. I say rendered because it is not

---

21   Riplinger, *New Age Bible Versions*, p. 319
22   Norman Geisler, *The Infiltration of the New Age* (Tyndale House Pub,1989) p. 142

really translated; it is transliterated from the Greek word Χριστός (Christos). Translated, Χριστός (Christos) becomes 'Anointed One' or 'Messiah.' You can see these different choices in one of Riplinger's examples of "the Christ" vs. "Christ." Here is Luke 4:41 in the KJV and two modern translations:

> KJV: And he said unto them, How say they that Christ is David's son?
> ESV: But he said to them, "How can they say that the Christ is David's son?"
> ISV: Then he asked them, "How can people say that the Messiah is David's son?"

When it comes to the word Χριστός (Christos), a translator must make two choices. The first is to treat it as a name or as a title. In English, names do not use the definite article (the), while titles normally do. We would say he was *the* President when referring to George Washington, but not *the* Washington. Second, the translator must decide between transliterating the word (KJV, ESV) or translating it (ISV). Neither of these choices shows any New Age Influence.

Since Cherry Picking only considers supporting evidence, it should not be surprising that conflicting evidence, such as the explanation above, is often ignored. Sometimes this is done by changing the subject, sometimes by raising a new claim. Often it will be with one of the other problems discussed in this or the next two chapters. But, one way or another, only supporting evidence is given any serious consideration.

Another area where this approach often occurs is in discussions over the Bible's teachings. Different verses are pitted against each other. This is a difficult area because there are times when it is legitimate to "use scripture to interpret scripture." For those who hold a high view of scripture, and particularly for those who hold to inerrancy, all parts of the Bible must agree if God both inspired the Bible and cannot contradict himself. When given two (or more) possible understandings of a passage, where one agrees with the rest of the Bible and another does not, the one that does not can legitimately be rejected.

An example of this is the NIV's translation of Hebrew 3:16, which reads, "Who were they who heard and rebelled? Were they not all those Moses led out of Egypt?" Some who believe only the KJV is the true word of God argue this conflicts with Numbers 14, which says that Joshua and Caleb did not rebel (Numbers 14:6-9). They argue that since Joshua and Caleb did not rebel; it was not "all those Moses led out of Egypt." Here, they claim, the NIV had introduced an error into the Bible.

The problem is that in ancient times, as now, "all" does not always mean absolutely every single one. Often 'all' is used for emphasis with a meaning of 'nearly all' or 'most.' In fact, it has the meaning of 'nearly all' in the very passage with which the NIV version of Hebrews 3:16 is supposed to conflict. The KJV translation of Numbers 14 begins, "And all the congregation lifted up their voice, and cried; and the people wept that night. And all the children of Israel murmured against Moses and against Aaron" (Numbers 14:1-2). There are two legitimate understandings of 'all' in Hebrews 3:16, one that leads to an error and one that does not. Given this, the choice is clear, and we should understand the passage in light of Numbers 14.

Notice, in this case, that we used scripture to decide between two possible understandings of a passage. The Cherry Picking approach comes into play when someone uses one scripture to ignore the teaching of another. For example, a common Jehovah's Witnesses' argument is, 'John 1:1 cannot say Jesus is God, because John 17:3 says that the Father is the only true God.' In this argument, John 17:3 is being used to ignore John 1:1.

This distinction between a legitimate "letting scripture interpret scripture," and Cherry Picking may seem subtle. There are times where the distinction is not clear. Still, it can be demonstrated by looking at what modification would be required to the Jehovah's Witnesses argument to make it a legitimate argument.

The Jehovah's Witnesses would have to show two things, to make a legitimate argument. The first is that their view of John 1:1 is a legitimate way to understand the verse, and second, that John 17:3 conflicts with the belief that Jesus is God.

There are two ways to translate the key part of John 1:1. The New World Translation, the translation used by Jehovah's Witnesses, renders the verse's last clause as "the Word was a god." While unlikely, this translation is grammatically possible. Other translations render this clause as "The Word was God." Still, even if one accepts that "a god" is the correct translation, there is a problem with the Jehovah's Witnesses' claim. The key problem Jehovah's Witnesses see in the standard translation is that it says Jesus is God. Yet, their translation of John 1:1 still says that Jesus is a god. While it avoids the normal translation, one that is in line with the doctrine of the Trinity, it does so at the expense of introducing polytheism. Jesus as "a god" would mean at least two gods.

Their translation not only conflicts with John 17:3 but all of the Old and New Testament teachings on the nature of God. To get around this problem, Jehovah's Witnesses go on to claim that "a god" does not actually mean a god, but only means that Jesus was divine. There is yet another problem with this claim, as there is a separate Greek word for 'divine' (θεῖος – theios). John could easily have said divine had he intended the meaning of 'divine,' but he didn't; he said God. So while their translation of John 1:1 is at least possible, their understanding of the passage is problematic at best.

This leaves the supposed conflict between the Trinitarian understanding of John 1:1 and John 17:3. Since the Trinity is monotheistic, there is no conflict from the Trinitarian point of view between Jesus being God in John 1:1 and the statement that the Father is God in John 17:3.

Looking at the Jehovah's Witnesses' claims, their translation of John 1:1 does not even solve the problem they are attempting to avoid in the common translation. They have to change the meaning of "was a god" to was "divine." At each point in this process, they pick that which best fits the goal they are trying to achieve.

The key to identifying the Cherry Picking approach is how a person deals with arguments and evidence that disagree with them. Do they directly confront and address the full force of the problem, or do they pick and choose among the option to get the results they want?

THE BOG

Closely related to the Cherry Picking approach is what I call the bog. All positions of any significance and complexity have problems. Let me be clear about this: ALL positions of any significance and complexity have problems. This is to be expected for the simple fact that we do not know everything. Thus major viewpoints are broken down into what (we think) we know and what we still need to work on. There will be things we do not know, things we cannot explain, questions we cannot answer. This lack of knowledge is why the search for knowledge is an ongoing process.

Those using the bog approach turns this normal situation on its head. It is a sort of reverse confirmation bias. When confronted with a viewpoint they reject, they ignore areas with solid reasons and evidence, focusing instead only on areas with some legitimate uncertainty. At the same time, they avoid those areas where the problems with their own position are clear. Think of a bog as fog-shrouded areas where the ground is uncertain. This uncertainly can make their position seem more viable than it is.

A great example of this is a series of discussions I had concerning monotheism and Psalm 82. Psalm 82 is one of the more troubling verses for monotheists. It is also a verse whose meaning is uncertain. The main difficulty in this Psalm is that God said to someone or something, "I said, 'you are gods'" (Psalm 82:6). To understand this verse, we first must answer several questions, such as, who is God referring to, and what does he mean when he calls them gods? A major difficulty is that Psalms are poetry, which allows for a much greater degree of allusion and allegory than prose. As a result, there are lots of theories about the meaning of this

Psalm. Ultimately we do not know. By itself, this passage could be understood in a way consistent with polytheism. There are also several possible ways of understanding this passage that are consistent with monotheism. Ultimately, there is no agreement among scholars over the meaning of this verse.[23]

I have talked to those who want to defend polytheism, or who at least want to reject monotheism, who are content discussing the few verses like Psalm 82. Our knowledge of the verse's context and background is uncertain; thus, no firm conclusion can be reached. At the same time, they are very reluctant to engage in discussions of the vastly more numerous passages clearly teaching there is only one God. Passages such as Deuteronomy 6:4 "Listen, Israel! The LORD is our God, the LORD alone"; 1 Kings 8:60 "so that, in turn, all the people of the earth may know that the LORD is God—there is no one else"; Isaiah 45:5 "I am the Lord, and there is no other; apart from me there is no God." Thus the key to the Bog is the desire to discuss only those areas where there is enough uncertainty that one's position is at least a possibility.

CONSPIRACY THEORY MENTALITY

One of the more disturbing trends in modern society is the growth of grand conspiracy theories. These theories spring up, giving alternate explanations for most major events. There are, for example, all the theories surrounding the assassination of John F. Kennedy. There are the claims we did not go to the moon, but rather it was all faked, or accusations that the government is hiding evidence of UFOs. There are warnings that the Trilateral Commission, Council on Foreign Relations, UN, or insert-name-

---

23   Some of the major suggestions for the identity of the 'gods' are: the judges of Israel, the generation who came out of Egypt, or the false gods of the nations surrounding Israel. The context of John 10 and Jesus' statement that the "Word of God came" to these "gods" would seem to support one of the first two options. The use of Elohim (the word translated gods in Psalm 82) in Exodus 22:8,9 and 1 Samuel 2:25 supports the belief these were judges.

of-a-group-you-don't-like, is trying to take over the world. These are just a few. Thus it is not surprising to find this type of thinking in the area of religion.

Large conspiracies rarely occur. The larger the alleged conspiracy, the less likely it is to be true because conspiracies depend on secrecy; it is hard to keep a secret. The bigger the secret, and the more people who know about the secret, the harder it is to keep.

The conspiracy theory mentality, however, has a deeper problem, which leads to its inclusion here. Grand conspiracy theories are so large they inevitably become what in logic is called a tautology. A tautology's technical definition is an argument that "is true under all possible interpretations of its variables."[24] In other words, a tautology is an argument constructed so that it is always true, no matter what.

While always being true may at first seem to be a good thing, what is distinctive about tautologies is that they are true no matter what; nothing can prove them false. As a result, they tell us nothing about the real world. This property of tautologies is illustrated with a simple example. The statement, "It is either cold or not cold," is a tautology. This statement will always be true, no matter the actual temperature. Yet, while true, it tells us nothing about the actual temperature. A weatherman saying, "It will be either cold or not cold today," is no help in determining whether or not you should take a coat!

Grand conspiracy theories fit into the category of tautologies. Any evidence not fitting the particular theory is written off as either being in error or, if that is not possible, as planted to divert attention away from the conspiracy. As such, they are immune to evidence and reason because there is a ready-made excuse to explain away anything disproving the theory. Just as the actual temperature is irrelevant to the statement "It is either cold or not cold," the actual evidence is irrelevant to grand conspiracy theories.

---

24 Charles W Kegley and Jacquelyn Ann Kegley, *Introduction to Logic* (Columbus, OH, Charles E. Merrill, 1978), p. 257

One of the more common areas where a conspiracy theory mentality comes into play is the origin of the Bible. The evidence for the reliability text of the Bible is very strong. It is so strong that there is really no reasonable doubt the texts used when translating modern Bibles are essentially the same as what the prophets and apostles wrote.[25] Yet, this evidence does not stop the numerous claims and charges of rewriting and suppression by some critics.

Some in the New Age movement, for example, claim the early church leaders removed the teaching of reincarnation from the Bible. That there is no evidence to support such claims and strong evidence against them is no problem. Supporters of such views claim the early church leaders suppressed all the evidence that would have supported their theory. As for the evidence that conflicts with their claims, the early church leaders planted that to mislead people. The key to the conspiracy theory mentality is that all evidence that might refute the theory is effectively ignored, i.e., it is part of the conspiracy.

SPECULATION AS EVIDENCE

The Speculation as Evidence approach confuses speculation with evidence and is often a major component in conspiracy theories. Speculation as Evidence begins innocently enough as mere speculation, speculations that later become the basis for conclusions. The problem enters when these conclusions are then treated as facts, facts that become the premises in further conclusions. Before long, you have a long and elaborate structure of seemingly reasonable arguments, which at its foundation is only speculation.

A good example of Speculation as Evidence can be found in the book "The Jesus Conspiracy" by Holger Kersten and Elmar Gruber. At its core, their book is another attempt to prove Jesus survived the Cross. His survival explains the accounts of the resurrection found in the Bible. Kersten and Gruber build much of

---

25   Elgin L Hushbeck, Jr, *Evidence for the Bible*, pp. 5-20

their theory upon the premise that Jesus belonged to a first-century Jewish sect called the Essenes.

Their style is Speculation as Evidence. First, Kersten and Gruber introduce something as a possibility. "Jesus was close to the sect of the Essenes, indeed it is likely that he belonged to a branch of the sect."[26] Before long, this speculation becomes fact. "John the Baptist was a *schaliach,* an apostle of the sect of Qumran," and "John was in a sense his spiritual director, and Jesus a disciple."[27]

Their evidence for this are the parallels they find between John and Jesus and the Essenes. Notice from the following passage how a reference to a similar word (desert) is built into elaborate detail:

> The recluses of Qumran refer in their writings to the area where they live as 'the desert.' This was where John lived, possibly in the Qumran caves; here Jesus withdrew for forty days and experienced the temptation by the devil (Luke 4:1-13). In Mark's Gospel it is said that Jesus 'was with the wild beasts; and the angels ministered unto him.' (Mark 1:13). The 'angels' or messengers of God were probably Essene monks, who supervised the 'novitiate' of Jesus in a cave outside of Qumran. [28]

The initial speculation that Jesus may have been an Essene is developed into an elaborate description of how Jesus was trained. Before long, that he was an Essene is taken as a fact.

Another example can be seen in their discussion of the drink given to Jesus while on the cross. They start by saying, "One can only speculate as to what the bitter fluid consisted of."[29] By the time they reach the next page, they are claiming,

> "Hence the effect of this drug was in many ways ideal for Joseph and his friend: not only was Jesus given the best of painkillers, the dose was designed to make him lose con-

---

26 Kersten and Gruber, *The Jesus Conspiracy* (Rockport, MA: Element, 1992) p. 238
27 Kersten, *Jesus*, pp. 239-240
28 Kersten, *Jesus*, p. 240
29 Kersten, *Jesus*, p. 253

sciousness in a short period of time so as to hang on the cross 'as if dead.'"[30]

At times, speculation can be difficult to spot, for the underlying speculation may be several layers deep in the argument. The key, however, is that the facts and speculations are so confused as to be indistinguishable.

DOUBLE STANDARD

Double standards are where the rules of evidence change depending on whether they are defending something they agree with or attacking something with which they disagree. While widespread, a good example is in the arguments of KJV-only supporters. For example, KJV-only supporters criticize the modern versions for being based on a minority of manuscripts, ignoring the majority of manuscripts. For example, Dr. Thomas Cassidy questions why modern scholars "throw out the evidence provided by the vast majority of manuscripts to follow only a small minority of texts?"[31] He stresses, "The Traditional Text of the Greek New Testament existed in the vast majority of Greek manuscripts."[32]

So far, this is a legitimate position to hold. When deciding between two readings, the best way to determine which reading was original and which was a later addition or mistake, is a legitimate question. There is room for disagreement. Yet, while a Majority Text view is legitimate, KJV-only supporters are not trying to defend the majority text. They are trying to defend the KJV. The problem begins when KJV-only supporters come to readings found in the KJV that are not supported by the majority of manuscripts. In these places, they have no problem at all, rejecting the majority in favor of the minority!

---

30   Kersten, *Jesus*, p. 254
31   Dr Thomas Cassidy, *Textual Criticism, Fact and Fiction: a fresh look at Bible Inspiration, Preservation And Translation* (http://www.aloha.net/~bstaggs/textcrit.txt)
32   Cassidy, *Textual*

Only four Greek manuscripts contain the entire passage of 1 John 5:7-8, as translated in the KJV, and the earliest of these manuscripts dates from the 14th century.[33] In addition to these four manuscripts, this passage was added to the text (i.e., written in the margins) in four other manuscripts[34]. Even if we include the four manuscripts where this passage was later added in the margins, the additional words found in the KJV exists in only eight Greek manuscripts. Thus the double standard. The majority of manuscripts are the standard only when being critical of the modern versions. The majority of manuscripts become irrelevant when looking at the KJV.

Ultimately, KJV-only supporters defend the KJV. The standard for judging shifts from passage to passage, based on whatever is needed to defend the KJV at that point. The rejection of the minority text is a clear example of the double standard because the minority reading is always defended if it happened to be in the KJV.

PARADIGM WARP

The most severe problem I have encountered is where one's view of reality is so wrapped up in the positions they hold that reality no longer seems to matter. For someone suffering from paradigm warp, the truth becomes that which supports what they believe, and error becomes that which does not support them.

I once encountered a mild case of paradigm warp with one of my first Sunday School teachers after becoming a Christian. He had come over to my house, and we were talking about his upcoming lesson. He had just heard about how NASA computers had discovered a day was missing. This discovery confirmed the account of the sun standing still in Joshua. I had encountered this story before and pointed out that it was not true. In fact, not only

---

33   mss 61 (1520); mss 2318 (1592); mss 629 (14th-16th century); mss 918 (16th century)

34   mss 221 (10th century); mss 635 (11th century); mss 88 (12th century); mss 429 (14th century)

was it false; it was impossible for the data does not exist that would permit such calculations.

For this story to be true, we would need accurate positions of the planets or events such as an eclipse on a given date from before the time of Joshua. If we had such data, NASA could then use this to calculate where the planets should be now and see that they were out of place by 24 hours.

The problem is that we have no such data. Ancient people did not use modern calendars. They considered a precise date to be more along the lines of 'in the springtime of the fourth year' of a given ruler. Even then, often, there is disagreement among scholars on the years that monarchs ruled. When we do find a record that mentions an event such as an eclipse, we calculate backward to date the record. So finding a missing day is simply impossible with the data we have.

After explaining this, he seemed to agree. Yet come Sunday morning, he told the class about this "new discovery." After class, I asked him why he had used the story when I had pointed out that it was false? He said that it confirmed the Bible, and since the Bible was true, it was just too good not to use.

If paradigm warp were not enough of a problem, since "truth" is whatever supports them, those who suffer from paradigm warp also fall victim to all the other problems discussed here and in the next two chapters. One sign of paradigm warp is the staunch defense of these errors (if it supports them, it must be true) and an attack on sound reasoning (if it disagrees with them, it must be false).

One of Paradigm Warp's interesting aspects is how it often uses a Conspiracy Theory Mentality to classify those who disagree. Those who disagree fall into one of three categories: the ignorant, the misled, and those who are, for lack of a better term, the enemy.

Normally when you first encounter Paradigm Warp, you will be assumed to be ignorant. When classed as the ignorant, the discussion proceeds in a fairly normal fashion. Still, if it becomes clear that you are already familiar with the subject or when you do not readily accept their "truth," then you are assumed to be part of the misled. The enemy has corrupted you, but there is still hope.

The dividing line between the misled and those who are the enemy is in how knowledgeable you are. If you are knowledgeable enough to effectively point out the errors in their position, you are the enemy. Being part of the enemy normally means you are part of some larger conspiracy to suppress the "truth." Your denials of being part of the grand conspiracy will, of course, be ignored. After all, as a member of the conspiracy, you could hardly be expected to do anything but deny it.

Paradigm warp becomes clear at this point because those involved are not dealing with reality, but with their distorted view of it. Often, someone in paradigm warp will not accept that you believe what you say you believe; they will think you believe what you are supposed to believe as someone who disagrees with their views. In extreme cases, I have even had people try to tell me about events in my life as if I had not been there, but they were!

While paradigm warp is the most severe problem, luckily, it is also not very common. The key to paradigm warp is the truth becomes whatever supports what a person believes, and error is that which does not.

In this chapter, we have seen a few of the more common ways in which evidence can be selected, ignored, or manipulated to lead to the desired conclusions. While they are presented here as individual errors, it is quite common to see them combined. For example, those who support grand conspiracies often built their theories on a combination of speculation (Speculation) and carefully selected evidence (Cherry Picking). Many like to concentrate on areas where there is uncertainty (the Bog) and hold conflicting points of view (Double Standard) to support their theories. Otherwise, they could never survive. In the next chapter, we will look at the types of uncritical thinking that deal more with the reasoning process and communication methods than with the actual evidence.

CHAPTER 6

NOT SO CRITICAL THINKING: COMMUNICATION

Do not let anyone deceive you with meaningless words, for it is because of these things that God becomes angry with those who disobey.
(Ephesians 5:6)

A key part of the reasoning process deals with testing one's position. Perhaps the best way to test a position is to try it on someone who disagrees. This inevitably involves communication. After all, it is normally much easier to find flaws in others' positions, positions you disagree with, than in your own positions. Because of this, discussion and debate are very important parts of the reasoning process. When you communicate your ideas in ways that limit others' ability to fully or honestly evaluate them, you have not really tested them. Faulty methods of communication can result in errors, just as faulty methods of evidence.

Let's look at an extreme case. Suppose a dictator made it a practice to have anyone who disagreed with them immediately shot. One day this dictator decided that because the sky was blue, therefore the earth was flat. To test his new theory, he asked if anyone could see a flaw with his thinking. Since no one stepped forward and attempted to refute him, he concluded that he was correct. Now it is pretty clear that the dictator's communication method, i.e., shooting those who disagree, would influence those who might have considered pointing out his error. As such, he had not tested his reasoning at all; rather, he tested the effectiveness of his threat.

While a somewhat extreme example, it demonstrates that communication problems can affect our ability to test our reasoning and conclusions. Granted, you are not likely to find yourself in such a situation, but more real-life examples are not too hard to imagine. Maybe you work for someone who will fire any who voiced a disagreement. Perhaps you know someone who responds to disagreement by increasing the volume of their voice rather than the cogency of their argument. Such people may very well think their reasoning sound, as no one disagrees. As such, we turn now to some other problems centered more around the presentation and defense of arguments than the evidence itself.

Many of these issues are much broader than how one deals with evidence discussed in the last chapter. They only become apparent over time as a discussion develops. To give particular examples for some of these issues would require the analysis of pages rather than sentences or paragraphs. As such, most of the examples in this chapter will be more general.

WINNING OVER TRUTH

One of the most common problems, and one that is most likely to affect those like me who regularly discuss controversial issues, is seeking to win more than seeking the truth. Ideally, the goal of all discussions, and particularly spiritual ones, should be to know the truth better, but we live in a fallen world. While defending a point of view, especially our own, it is difficult not to get so caught up in the discussion that the main goal becomes winning the debate. Sometimes the direction a discussion takes is more determined by strategies and counter-strategies aimed at scoring points rather than determining what is true.

Examples of winning over truth are not easy to give because it only becomes apparent after some discussion. Even then, it is not always clear. In addition, this frequently involves the motives behind a particular argument rather than the argument itself. For example, is someone using Bog arguments because they don't know any better? Or are they doing so as a tactical strategy, knowing it is the only way they can defend their position?[35]

In the heat of a discussion, it is very easy to get caught up with the desire to win. Still, one key to winning over truth is the ability to admit error and correct arguments. One thing we can be sure of is that, other than God, no one is perfect; no one has an all perfect knowledge of the truth. We all make mistakes. I often have had to refine my arguments as people raise points or questions I have not considered or have pointed out flaws in my thinking.

Several times I have come up with what seemed to me at the time to be a killer argument, an argument so good that it will leave my opponent speechless. Yet the first time I tried to use them, my opponent quickly pointed out how I had forgotten some key piece of evidence or had missed a flaw in my reasoning. As a result, my devastating argument was immediately, completely, and utterly shot down, and I was the one who was left speechless. A good dose of humility is very important if the goal of a discussion is the truth.

In extreme cases, someone with a winning-over-truth mentality will not concede even the slightest error, no matter how blatant it is. A common response, especially in online discussions, is the "tactical retreat," i.e., they end the discussion when it becomes apparent that they are in an indefensible position. A tactical retreat is not always a bad thing. Sometimes the best answer will be, 'that is a good point; let me look into it and get back to you.' Still, the

---

35 This raises the question of why would someone defend a position they knew to be so weak? Usually, it is because they accept the position on other grounds. For example, Mormons believe that the Holy Spirit has personally communicated to them that Joseph Smith was a true prophet of God. Now a Mormon might realize the evidence is completely against the Book of Abraham being what Joseph Smith claimed it was, but to reject this would be to reject that Joseph Smith was a prophet. Therefore Mormons often see this as a question of whether they will believe the evidence, or will they believe the Holy Spirit? This is why they tend to avoid such discussions in the first place, but if they do try to defend the book of Abraham, they have little choice but to engage in strategies such as the Winning over Truth.

key to winning over truth is making winning the debate a higher goal than coming to the truth.

EMOTIONAL APPEALS

We are not intelligent robots but human beings with emotions. As a result, emotional appeals can be very effective. They can also be some of the most misleading arguments when not tempered by reason. The exact line between legitimate and illegitimate in terms of an emotional appeal is not always easy to draw. Perhaps the best guideline is the correlation between the emotions being appealed to and the situation's reality.

Emotional appeals driving home the magnitude and horror of the mass murders under the totalitarian regimes of Nazi Germany, the Soviet Union, China under Mao, or Cambodia during the 1970s are completely justified. Such evil cannot be fully comprehended simply by reason alone. On the other hand, similar emotional appeals protesting the slowing of a government aid program's growth by likening them to such holocausts would not be legitimate.

The importance of such appeals becomes apparent in the battles that occur over labels. Groups will normally label themselves so that people will react to their name. While a few may seek negative reactions, for most groups, the reaction sought is positive. Thus in the abortion debate, the major sides refer to themselves as "Pro." One side is "Pro-choice," and the other is "Pro-Life."

Just as one label can elicit positive reactions, a different label can elicit a negative response. Because of this, groups rarely stop at labeling themselves and seek to label their opponents. Pro-choice supporters often label their opponents "Anti-choice," and Pro-Life supporters label their opponents as "Pro-abortion." By their very nature, such arguments over labels are not reasoned defenses of a position, rather an attempt to control people's emotional reaction to a name. The importance of such arguments to the outcome of political battles is a good indicator of the lack of rational thought in modern society.

Appeals to emotions are not, in and of themselves, arguments or evidence for a position. Correctly used emotional appeals should emphasize a position, not distort or justify it. In my classes, I normally liken emotional arguments to salt. Just as adding a little salt can improve a food's flavor, an emotional appeal can highlight and emphasize a rational argument. However, just as too much salt can ruin a dish, too much emotion can overwhelm an argument. The key question is when you remove the emotion, is there any rational argument left?

BOMB THROWING

One of the more difficult tactics to deal with is a special type of emotional appeal I call Bomb Throwing. This tactic is difficult because much of the Bomb Thrower's arguments center around emotionally loaded language, language designed to make people react rather than think. I refer to it as Bomb Throwing because I have seen many rational discussions completely break down when a bomb-thrower jumps in.

This is the leading tactic of Trolls, one of the banes of the Internet. Trolls enter a discussion, throw around a few outrageous charges, and then sit back and watch people react. There is no dealing with them except to ignore them, and thus the well known saying, "Don't Feed the Trolls." They aim their arguments more at disrupting and sidetracking a discussion rather than advancing it.

Often bomb-throwing is little more than argument-by-adjective or simply name-calling. An excellent example of this is Dr. Peter S. Ruckman's response to James White's list of seven KJV translators' errors. Rather than just defending the KJV and showing where White was in error, Ruckman attacks White and his position in virtually every paragraph with section headers such as: "Bugs Bunny in Wonderland;" "C'mon, Buster, tell us. You got the balloons;" and comments like, "This is an error, according to Jimbo;"

"He is so screwed up he doesn't know whether he is standing on his left hind leg or his front right paw;" "You silly smart-aleck little Twinkies!" "Flimsy-Jimmy," etc.[36]

Such language creates an atmosphere, especially in public discussions, where any actual intelligent discussion of issues is virtually impossible – which frankly is often the point. After all, if you so disrupt the discussion that no rational points can be made, you do not have to deal with your position's problems. It also allows one to make seemingly strong points out of nothing. Consider the following portion of Ruckman's reply:

> Now James White – an absolutely typical Alexandrian clone – was programmed by the same "good, godly, Conservative JACKASSES" that tried to program me. I don't "program" too well. So when old Jimmy wrote his book, he made a vain attempt to handle the "gender" problem of Nestle, Aland, Metzger, Fee, Palmer, Barker, Bob Jones III, Custer, Afman, Panosian, Wisdom, Ross, Sandlin, Kutilek, Brunner, and Brokenshire, et al., on three neuter words taking a masculine article as masculine witnesses he stumbled, stuttered, and then bluffed his way through the passage without explaining anything.
>
> Dr. Edward Hills had already nailed Jimbo to the wall way back in 1956[37]: that was thirty-nine years before Jimbo wrote *The King James Only Controversy.*[38]

While at first reading, this may seem like a strong critique of White's argument, note that it is little more than blustering insults upon closer inspection. Ruckman refers to White's argument concerning the additional words found in the KJV translation of 1 John 5: 7-8 discussed in Chapter 5, and his response is full of the problems discussed in these chapters. White and others point

---

36   Dr. Peter S. Ruckman, *James White's Seven Errors in the King James Bible - Errors 6 & 7* (Bible Believers' Bulletin, March 1996)
____https://www.tapatalk.com/groups/av1611godsword/viewtopic.php?f=2&t=940 (Retrieved April 10, 2020)

37   Cited by Ruckman: Dr. Edward Hills, *The King James Version Defended,* 1956, pp. 209-213

38   Ruckman, *James*

out that the additional words appear in only a few late Greek manuscripts. Ruckman tried to claim they are liars and cites other translations and allusions to support his case. Yet it only an apparent refutation. That the additional words appear in, for example, the Latin Vulgate is well known and does not invalidate White's claim about the Greek manuscripts.

Keeping the focus on Bomb Throwing, he rejects White's position saying, "he stumbled, stuttered, and then bluffed his way through the passage without explaining anything." Then he refers the reader to another source again without giving any details to back him up, other than to claim he somehow "nailed Jimbo to the wall." These are not reasons; these are simply Ruckman's opinions disguised as reasons. While it is abundantly clear that Ruckman disagrees with White, he has given the reader little to back up his rejection other than a lot of emotionally loaded language.

While all groups are susceptible to bomb-throwing, it has been my experience, the level of emotionally loaded language is inversely proportional to the strength of the argument. In other words, the less evidence there is to support a position, the more likely you are to encounter emotionally-loaded language. This should not be too surprising. It is easy to present the evidence and let it speak for itself when the evidence is solidly on your side. However, if there is little or no evidence, or even worst, the evidence is against you, you must look to other means to defend your position. As with the adage for lawyers: If the facts support you, argue the facts. If the law supports you, argue the law. If neither supports you, yell a lot.

Emotionally loaded language may be the only way to maintain their belief for those whose position is baseless. This is especially true if they believe their own rhetoric. It is very difficult for opponents to deal with, and it is also self-reinforcing. After all, if you believe your opponents to be ignorant clones, then why believe them or any evidence they give you? Also, few will discuss such issues with them as their emotionally loaded language makes any rational discussion difficult.[39]

Often, bomb-throwers make a big deal out of how those with differing opinions refuse to debate them. Unlike the dictator in the story at the beginning of this chapter, they do not shoot those who disagree. Still, the effect of their emotionally loaded language on suppressing criticism is pretty much the same; few will challenge them. As a result, they have effectively insulated themselves from any conflicting opinion.

The key to the bomb-thrower is not that difficult. If you are dealing with someone who, instead of a reasoned analysis of the evidence, responds with emotionally loaded language, language aimed at attacking or ridiculing you personally, you are dealing with a bomb thrower.

FORCED IGNORANCE

One of the more frustrating approaches I have encountered is what I call Forced Ignorance. This problem occurs when the person you are discussing with can never quite seem to understand your point no matter how you make it. This is not a question of intelligence. I have encountered some very intelligent people with this problem. Nor am I talking about agreeing with an argument. Forced ignorance occurs when a person does not grasp the basic argument so that they can respond.

Force Ignorance can result from two possibilities. The first and the most common is what might be called Reactive Forced Ignorance. Reactive Forced Ignorance occurs when the person does not respond to the arguments or evidence presented but instead reacts to certain words or phrases. As such, they probably would understand the argument if they ever took the time to try.

---

39 I have attempted this a few times in online discussions. The main problem is the strong temptation to respond in kind. More then once, I have written a reply only to delete the whole thing and start again after "cooling down."

For example, in a discussion, I once pointed out that an argument was flawed because it used circular reasoning. In doing so, I gave an example that demonstrated the circular nature of the argument. Rather than address the actual example I gave, the response was that the argument was fine. It was, in fact, my arguments that were circular. The person then proceeded to show me how I was guilty of circular reasoning.

Now at this point, their response could be Tu Quoque, a fallacy we will look at in the next chapter. In terms of Forced Ignorance, his example distorted my position, showing he did not understand it. An even bigger problem was that his example of my "circular reasoning" was not even circular! After several attempts to explain what a circular argument was, it became very clear that he was not attempting to figure out what I was saying. Instead, he was merely responding to certain words and phrases.

The other type of forced ignorance is much harder to label. The person reacts to the individual parts of an argument but still never quite seems to get the overall point you are making. While I have never experienced this in a face to face discussion, I have encountered this a few times in online discussions. Thus, it is hard to say whether this is simply a problem with online discussions or with a person so locked into a given paradigm that it is impossible for them even to see alternatives. Perhaps it is just easier to pretend not to understand when responding electronically.

One thing that is central about Forced Ignorance is that it is fundamentally a breakdown of communication. Communication requires a minimum of two people. Thus an important consideration here is that the problem is probably not with others if everyone who disagrees with you seems to have a bad case of Forced Ignorance. The key here is the inability or unwillingness to understand the basic argument you are making. To be Forced Ignorance, it must be an argument that you have successfully communicated to others who have disagreed in the past.

RECYCLING ARGUMENTS

Recycling Arguments is that type of thinking that never seems to get very far beyond the initial response. In normal discussions, there will be an initial claim of some sort (C_1) followed by a response (R_1). The person making the first claim will then comment on the response (C_2), which will result in a second response (R_2), and so on as follows:

$$(C_1) \rightarrow (R_1) \ (C_2) \rightarrow (R_2) \rightarrow (C_3) \rightarrow (R_3) \ ... \ (C_n) \rightarrow (R_n)$$

In theory, the discussion proceeds until the sides reach an agreement, which may be that they agree to disagree. These discussions can often be very enjoyable as they grow and develop, branching into new areas, considerations, or subject matter. Even when such discussions do not end in agreement, they can still be very valuable. They can lead to a better understanding of the complexity and nuances of one's beliefs, along with a better understanding of those who disagree.

Recycling Arguments occur when one side stops responding and begins repeating points that were already made and addressed or asking questions already answered. Normally this happens very early in the discussion, and often by simply repeating the initial claim as if repeating it often enough will somehow make it true. Thus rather than the orderly progression we saw before, these discussions often go as follows:

$$(C_1) \rightarrow (R_1) \ (C_2) \rightarrow (R_2) \rightarrow (C_1) \rightarrow (R_3) \ ... \ (C_1) \rightarrow (R_n)$$

One group where I have frequently encounter this type of response is with Jehovah's Witnesses. Those I have encountered were normally very good at defending their beliefs, for example, their rejection of the Trinity as detailed in Watchtower literature. Often they could quote the watchtower arguments virtually word for word. As the discussion progresses beyond that found in Watchtower literature, most of those I have spoken with suddenly went back and began simply repeating points we had already covered. You are probably facing this problem if you constantly return to points, points you thought were settled, or at least addressed.

RECYCLING CONCLUSIONS

The reverse of Recycling Arguments is, not too surprisingly, Recycling Conclusions. We live in a complex world, and our beliefs about the world are correspondingly complex. For example, the scientific equation $E=mc^2$ may be a very simple equation. Still, the underlying reasoning and evidence that led Einstein to reach this conclusion are not. The conclusions we have reached result from many other conclusions and assumptions, in a long train of reasoning that goes back much farther than most people realize.

Often, differences of opinion are not the result of one side looking at the evidence while the other does not. More often than not, it is that both sides make different assumptions and thus evaluate the evidence in different ways. As we stated in Chapter 4, any rational discussion must first establish common ground. Those caught up in Recycling Conclusions only want to focus on the conclusions they argue and not the underlying assumptions that back them up.

I have often encountered this problem with atheists who assume a completely naturalistic worldview. Everything must be explained by science in such a worldview, and nothing supernatural is allowed to exist. It is no wonder that they find no convincing evidence for the existence of the supernatural or God. Their world view does not permit it. Recycling Conclusions has come into play a few times when I have tried to discuss the problems with their underlying assumptions. Rather than defend them, these atheists simply ignored the problems I raised.

Take, for example, the claim that we can only know things through science. Sometimes, this claim is buried as an underlying assumption of demands that I present evidence within certain guidelines. A demand that I only present scientific evidence for God's existence. Often those making the demands do not want to discuss whether or not these demands are valid or reasonable.

While not all atheists or agnostics would make such a claim, I have run into many who did. At first blush, such a claim seems reasonable. Science is the best way we have discovered for learning how the world works. Still, there is a big gap between that statement and the claim that science is the only way we can know. It is a big leap even to go from science is the best way to the only way. If nothing else, there are all the other aspects of life. Do we only know about history or love because of science?

When someone claims science is the only way to know, I ask them how they know that claim is true? How do they know that science is the only way to know anything? Is it because science says science is the only way? The response takes many forms, but ultimately the claim is unsupportable. While, in theory, those claiming knowledge only comes through science could reject it, I have yet to see that happen. As a result, at some point, it will just be dogmatically restated, as if repetition somehow equated with justification.

Thus the key to Recycling Conclusions is that it avoids discussing the underlying assumptions that make up an assertion. They are simply stated and restated as firm conclusions.

THE SHELL GAME

The Shell Game is quite simple; you simply change the subject under discussion before any conclusion can be reached. Sometimes the change is only slight; sometimes, the issues raised are completely different. I was once in a discussion with a man who was trying to point out errors in the modern translations. About the time I felt I had pretty much refuted his claim, he would raise a new group of errors, and we would discuss these claims for a short period. Each time, he would give me another group of alleged problems, and I would address them, point by point. In and of itself, this was fine until he suddenly began recycling problems we had already dealt with as if they were brand new.

I asked him to pick what he thought was a problem, and we would discuss this alleged problem until he either made his point or withdrew it. He picked the alleged factual error between Hebrews 3:16 and Number 14 in the NIV discussed in chapter five. We had only been discussing this a short time when he began trying to change the subject once again. Next, he tried shifting the discussion away from the issue of the alleged factual error to one of whether or not the NIV version of this verse was a good translation. Finally, he tried to accuse me of changing the subject to one of the alleged factual errors! The key to the shell games is when the subject under discussion frequently changes without any resolution on individual points.

This chapter has looked at how the discussion and debate of an issue can lead to error. Again, as with the previous chapter, while these are presented here as individual problems, often, they are used in combination. It may be someone's strategy (Winning over Truth) to use emotionally loaded language (Bomb Throwing) as they distort the point you are making. Your attempts to clarify your position is ignored (Forced Ignorance) as they bombard you with new charges faster than you can respond (Shell Game). In the next chapter, we will turn to some of the more formalized errors: logical fallacies.

Chapter 7

Logical Fallacies

Test everything, hold on to the good. (1 Thessalonians 5:21)

In the last two chapters, we looked at some general approaches that are likely to lead to errors. In this chapter, we will look at some of the more common classical logical fallacies. While recognized as erroneous reasoning for thousands of years, it does not mean that they are of only historical interest. Quite the contrary, most of these you will encounter on a daily basis.

Attacking the Person (Ad Hominem)

Perhaps the most common logical fallacy of all is attacking the person instead of the argument. This fallacy occurs every day and in almost every area of life where there are differences of opinion. It is so common it can be subdivided into at least five major subforms: Abusive, Tu Quoque, Irrationality, Hypocrisy, and Motives\Bias.

Abusive

Perhaps the most common attack against the person is the abusive form. This fallacy is very similar to Bomb Throwing, except here attack need not be emotional. These usually come in a fashion similar to "You can't believe them, they are a _____" where you fill in the blank with some group or label you don't like. You can see this in Nathaniel's response to Phillip. Phillip came to Nathaniel and told him, "We have found the man about whom

Moses in the Law and the Prophets wrote—Jesus, the son of Joseph, from Nazareth." (John 1:45-6) Nathaniel responded, "From Nazareth? Can anything good come from there?" This rejection was not based on anything but from where Jesus came. Luckily, Philip was able to persuade him to come anyway.

This ad hominem attack is often nothing more than argument-by-label rather than by evidence and often uses emotionally loaded language. Also, this type of argument is one that Christians especially should always avoid. We are all children of God, and we are all sinners saved by grace. We should love the sinner but hate the sin; we should likewise love the person and deal with the argument.

Ad hominem attacks fall into the broader category of Fallacies of Irrelevance. It falls into this category because an argument's soundness comes from the premises and reasoning, not the person. The person making the argument is irrelevant. For example, it is completely irrelevant who makes the argument that:

All humans are mortal.

The apostle Paul was human.

Therefore the apostle Paul was mortal.

This is a valid deductive argument whose premises are true, so this argument will be sound regardless of who makes it.

Tu Quoque

Tu Quoque (pronounced Two-Quo-Key) is Latin for "you're another." This ad hominem attack responds to a charge, not by refuting the charge, but instead by making the same or similar charge in return. On several occasions, I have pointed out that a person's arguments were false because they were circular. Rather than responding by attempting to show how their arguments were not circular, they instead responded by claiming, "well, your arguments are also circular."

The strange thing about Tu Quoque responses is they, at best, only show both sides are wrong. As such, they are an admission of error. In reality, this is an attempt to change the focus away from their problems. Those using Tu Quoque claiming my arguments were circular would be quite happy if I forgot about the circularity I had just pointed out and instead defended myself. Anything to keep the focus off of their error.

Irrationality

The Irrationality form of ad hominem attack is a little harder to see when changing the subject. It occurs when the other person claims your arguments are unworthy of consideration because you hold other different but irrational beliefs. The claim of irrationality is made with the implication, implicit or explicit, that your current claims are likewise irrational. An interesting aspect of this fallacy is that the claim of irrationality may not even be grounded in something you believe. Rather, it is something that your opponent thinks you are supposed to believe.

I will often present the Cosmological argument when talking with atheists or agnostics, which I believe to be a very solid and good argument. One of the reasons I believe this argument works so well is skeptics often try to change the subject to the belief in a flat earth or a literal 7-day creation. In short, they try to move the discussion away from the cosmological argument and to a subject where they believe they are on more solid ground, or at least more comfortable.

That Christians once believed the earth was flat is more a myth created by Washington Irving than any historical view held by Christians. Irving, better known as the creator of Rip Van Winkle, wrote a popular history of Spain. In that history, he included a fanciful story of Columbus arguing against believers in a flat earth to make his voyage. Yet Columbus's detractors did not argue the earth was flat. They, like all educated people of the time, knew it to be round. Rather, they believed that Columbus was underestimating the size of the earth. They believed the earth was so large, the ocean between Europe and Asia so vast, that Columbus would be unable to sail across it before running out of food and water.

In one of the ironies of history, Columbus was wrong, and his critics were correct, at least on the earth's size. Outside of a few Vikings, no one knew that you encounter North and South America long before reaching Asia when sailing west from Europe. Columbus encountered land just before his crew was going to force him to turn around. The land he sighted was the Americas, not Asia. Columbus never realized his mistake and died believing he had reached Asia. Still, because of Washington Irving, skeptics have falsely accused Christians of believing in a flat earth since the early 1800s.

When critics try to switch to a literal 7-day creation, they try to change the subject to a related topic and a belief some Christians hold. Still, they are attempting to change the subject, and this falls into this fallacy. When the Cosmological argument is accepted, it only shows that something beyond the natural world is responsible for its existence. It does not by itself even show that God is responsible. It only shows that something beyond the natural is responsible. Other arguments are required to go further, and the Cosmological argument is just a first step. Yet even that step is too much for many atheists and agnostics whose entire worldview [38] is based on the belief there is only the natural universe. Accepting the cosmological argument would undermine that core and foundational belief. Thus they try to divert attention away from the actual argument and onto something, anything else.

The Cosmological argument is consistent with a belief in a literal 7-day creation. Still, it does not demand it. There are Christians who accept the Cosmological argument but who do not believe in a literal 7-day creation. I am one of them. Thus when they try to change the subject to this belief, it is not even one I accept. Whether one believes in a young earth or old earth, the attempt to avoid the Cosmological argument by claiming another belief is irrational is illogical. That makes this a fallacy.

Hypocrisy

Closely related to the fallacy of Irrationality is the fallacy of Hypocrisy. This fallacy occurs whenever there is an attempt to refute a claim by arguing the person making it is a hypocrite. Countering an argument with a charge of hypocrisy is a fallacy even if the charge is true. The person may very well be a hypocrite, but that does not mean the argument they are making is wrong or that we should reject it.

For example, a person using illegal drugs while arguing illegal drugs are terrible, destroying a person's life, might legitimately be called a hypocrite.[40] Yet this does not address the argument they are making. In fact, a drug addict's struggles and experiences could even give their arguments more weight. We are all sinners, saved by grace, and thus to some extent, we are all hypocrites. The Hypocrisy fallacy is yet another way of attempting to change the subject. It attempts to change the subject away from the argument and on to the person making the argument. It is another form of ad hominem attack.

For Christians, there is a potential problem with Hypocrisy being considered a fallacy. If it is a fallacy, and therefore irrational, what about those times when Jesus called people hypocrites? Was he irrational? Was he wrong to do so? The simple answer is no, and by looking at two examples of where Jesus did call people hypocrites, we can better understand this fallacy.

In Matthew 7, Jesus says, "You hypocrite, first take the log out of your own eye, and then you will see clearly to take the speck out

---

40 The validity of such an accusation would depend on the exact meaning of the word hypocrite. For some, hypocrite has a more restrictive meaning of, it is ok for me, but not for you. "It is ok for me to smoke, but your should not smoke." For others, the term is used in a boarder sense of something one does regardless of whether it is viewed as ok. "Smoking is bad and I wish I could quit. You should not start." An even broader sense would include something done in the past, which the person now condemns, such as a former smoker, now arguing smoking is bad. The point here is that the definition used does not affect whether this is a fallacy.

of your brother's eye." The first thing to note here is that Jesus was teaching, not countering an argument. He is not using the charge of hypocrisy to avoid some argument being made by his opponents but warning people about judging others. The point he was making is if something is so wrong you are condemning others, why are you not condemning yourself? The charge of hypocrisy is completely logical and appropriate here and is not a fallacy. Using a charge of hypocrisy when attempting to avoid an argument is a fallacy. Pointing out that someone is a hypocrite is not.

The situation in Mathew 15 is more difficult; Jesus is answering critics when he says of them, "you hypocrites!" Why is this not a fallacy? It is important to know both the nature of charge that the Pharisees and Scribes made against Jesus, along with the entirety of Jesus' response. If "you hypocrites!" had been all that He said, then it would have been a fallacy, but it was not.

The Pharisees and Scribes asked Jesus, "Why do your disciples break the tradition of the elders? For they do not wash their hands when they eat" (v 1-2). They referred to the rules for the ceremonial washing of hands, and Jesus' response has two major components, a mostly private one and a public one. Jesus directed the first part of his response, mostly private, directly to the Pharisees and Scribes. It was a charge of hypocrisy: "why do you break the commandment of God for the sake of your tradition?" (v 3) When making a general charge like this, it is often important to follow up with an example, which he does in verses 4-6. These verses give the basis for his charge of hypocrisy.

Jesus' response might have been the fallacy of Hypocrisy if he had stopped there, but he didn't. In the first part of his response, he laid the groundwork for his answer to their question. He summed up his example of their hypocrisy with, "So for the sake of your tradition you have made void the word of God" (v 6). The second part of Jesus' response was directed to the crowd at large,

> And he called the people to him and said to them, "Hear and understand: it is not what goes into the mouth that de-

files a person, but what comes out of the mouth; this defiles a person." (v10-11)

Thus Jesus did not use the charge of hypocrisy as a way of changing the subject or avoiding the argument the Pharisees and Scribes made; he answered it directly. His argument consists of the following points.

- First, the word of God is more important than the traditions of men. Thus, the rule to ceremonially wash your hands, as part of men's traditions, is not as important as the word of God.
- Second, they were included among the people about whom Isaiah spoke when he said, "This people honors me with their lips, but their heart is far from me; in vain do they worship me, teaching as doctrines the commandments of men." A charge of hypocrisy, true, but one that emphasized their "traditions of the elders" was not as important as God's commands. It also pointed out their faith in the "traditions of men" was misplaced.
- Third, what goes into one's mouth, in this case, a hand that had not been purified with a ceremonial ritual, does not defile a person. This response directly answered their question.

There is no fallacy here. Jesus does not use the charge to ignore the Pharisees and Scribes' question, but as a component in addressing it. Even without the charge of hypocrisy, Jesus addresses their argument.

Still, if the charge of hypocrisy was not needed, why did Jesus make it? First, while the major part of his refutation came as a teaching to the entire crowd, Jesus made the charge of hypocrisy directly to the Pharisees and Scribes. He was challenging their assumptions and giving them the chance to see their error. Some, like Nicodemus, did come to see their error and accepted Jesus' teachings.

Second, the Pharisees and Scribes were authority figures for the Jewish people. Above, I described this part of Jesus' response as mostly private. While he was talking directly to them, this was still a public setting. After all, there were people there he could call over to hear the public part of his response. Undoubtedly others witnessed the exchange, so by making the charge, Jesus was pointing out they were not the authority figures who could be trusted that they claimed to be.

Ultimately not all charges of hypocrisy are fallacious. However, when using a charge of hypocrisy to divert the discussion or ignore an argument, it should be rejected for the error that it is.

Motives\Bias

The final type of ad hominem argument attacks the motives of a person or their bias. I once discussed with a fairly liberal scholar who wrote off every conservative view as simply the result of "bias." Frankly, it became quite annoying. I would write a couple of pages of detailed arguments, and his response would be little more than "that's a biased view." He never pointed out what was wrong with the evidence I cited or wrong with my reasoning. All this was effectively ignored, with the claim of bias; that was a sufficient refutation for him.

By now, the problem with such an approach should be plain. This scholar ignored the evidence I presented and the arguments I made. Instead, he tried to change the focus of attention onto me. This problem is similar to the fallacy of hypocrisy. The charge may very well be true, but it is irrelevant. That I may be bias or a hypocrite does not say anything about the argument I am making. Arguments succeed or fail based on the evidence and reason supporting them, not on the person making the argument.

There is a further problem with this fallacy. How does one defend against a charge of bias? The only real way is to show that the evidence and arguments drive your conclusions, not your bias. Yet, given that this fallacy ignores evidence and arguments with the appeals to motives, or a charge of bias, any refutation becomes effectively impossible. Like many others, this fallacy is dangerous to use if truth is your goal, as its use insulates you from the best means for correcting your errors.

Things are complicated with this fallacy as the charge of bias is different from the other ad hominem attacks. There are times when it is not a fallacy to point to bias as a reason to question a person's claims. When a person's claim depends significantly on their judgment, as opposed to just reason and evidence, a charge of bias can be legitimate. This possibility of bias is why the Bible calls on judges to be fair and impartial.

> You are not to be unjust in deciding a case. You are not to
> show partiality to the poor or honor the great. Instead, decide
> the case of your neighbor with righteousness. (Leviticus 19:15)

It would be perfectly fine to point out when a judge demonstrates partiality to one side or the other. Such bias is a reason to question their ruling. The key distinction between a proper charge of bias and a fallacious one is whether the claim in question is based on reason and evidence or based on the person's judgment. It would be legitimate to raise the issue of motive if a defendant claims they are innocent because they were at home with their wife at the time. Is the wife truthful, or is she protecting her husband? Such an approach is not an ad hominem attack because it is directly addressing the evidence; in this case, the truthfulness of the wife's testimony.

For some, this distinction between a legitimate "attack" and a fallacious one is confusing. In reality, it is not all that difficult. It is legitimate to raise questions about the person's possible bias when the validity of a claim depends on the person making the argument. It is not legitimate to raise questions about bias when a claim's validity can be determined independently of the person. In short, you can raise questions about the person when the person is the evidence.

If I claim there is something more than the natural world because I have experienced it, questions about my bias would be legitimate. Except in rare circumstances, experiencing the super-natural is subjective. On the other hand, if I make the cosmological argument for the existence of something beyond the natural world,[41] raising questions about my "bias" as a Christian would not be legitimate. The Cosmological Argument stands or falls based on the evidence and reason, not on the person making the argument.

It may be a legitimate observation that, as a Christian, I find the argument more convincing. Still, one could equally observe that an atheist or agnostic is less likely to find it convincing. Note, these are observations about whether or not a person finds the argument convincing, not about the argument itself.

The five types of Ad Hominem attack, Abusive, Tu Quoque, Irrationality, Hypocrisy, and Motives\Bias, all have one key error at their core. They all ignore the argument and instead try to change the focus to the person making the argument.

INCONSISTENCY

The fallacy of inconsistency occurs when arguments have conflicting premises. Since the premises conflict with each other, they cannot all be correct, and therefore the conclusion cannot be sound. The most common type of inconsistent arguments I encounter occurs when people cite others' conclusions to support their point. Yet, the underlying premises for these conclusions are ones they would reject.

A major difference between the Mormon view of God and the view historically held by both Christians and Jews is Henotheism vs. Monotheism. Mormons believe that while we worship only one God, many gods exist, a view called henotheism, the belief in many, but the worship of one. Historically Christians and Jews are monotheists, believing we worship one God because there is only one God.

---

41 The cosmological argument starts with existence based on cause and effect and argues based on this that God exists. See *Christianity and Secularism*, pp. 59-66 for a more in-depth presentation of the argument.

A major problem for Mormons is that while there are numerous clear and direct statements of monotheism found throughout the Bible, there are no similarly clear statements of polytheism. Some Mormons cite scholars who claim the Hebrew scriptures' monotheism developed out of the surrounding religions' polytheism to support their belief. These scholars claim traces of the older polytheism still exist in the early books.

This line of reasoning has several problems. First, the scholars who claim such a development did occur still agree that later Judaism was strongly monotheistic. As such, these arguments reflect a strong Cherry Picking approach on the part of the Mormon attempting this line of reasoning. They pick out only those pieces of the scholar's work that support what they want to believe. More importantly, for this discussion, they are also inconsistent. The scholars who believe monotheism developed from polytheism base this on a view where religion is a human creation that changes and evolves to meet society's needs. Yet this is a view of religion Mormons reject. They believe true religion comes from God, not from society. As such, they reject the foundation for the conclusions they wish to use. This inconsistency renders their arguments invalid.

STRAWMAN

An argument very similar to the Irrationality form of ad hominem is the strawman. A strawman occurs when, instead of attacking the actual argument or claim, a different argument is attacked as if it was the original argument. Often, the original argument is distorted or exaggerated, but in ways that make it untenable. It is then the untenable version that is attacked and refuted. Metaphorically, they create a man of straw, which is much easier to defeat than a real opponent.

A good example of a strawman argument is Richard Dawkins' depiction of God found in his book *The God Delusion*[42]. In Chapter

---

42 Richard Dawkins, *The God Delusion* (Houghton Mifflin, 2006)

Two of that book, Dawkins turns to the question of God, starting the chapter with,

> The God of the Old Testament is arguably the most un-
> pleasant character in all the fiction: jealous and proud of it;
> a petty, and unjust, unforgiving control-freak; a vindictive,
> bloodthirsty ethnic cleanser; misogynistic, homophobic, racist,
> infanticidal, genocidal, filicidal, pestilential, megalomaniac,
> sadomasochistic, capriciously malevolent bully.

Dawkins' main justification for this statement is not any detailed scholarly analysis. Rather, Winston Churchill's son, Randolph, came to a similar conclusion when he read the Old Testament for the first time while in the army. Dawkins goes on to write, "It is unfair to attack such an easy target." Here Dawkins is correct. This view of God is one I doubt any believing Jew or Christian holds. The reason it is an easy target is that Dawkins created it to be so. This view is not an accurate depiction of God or what believers claim about God. He created a strawman view of God so that he can then knock it down easily. As a result, he is not dealing with reality.

If you are going to refute an argument, you must deal with the argument. You cannot attack some artificial argument designed specifically to be refuted. Yet, it is surprising how often I must spend time correcting misperceptions about what I supposedly believe. For example, it is quite common for Christians to be labeled anti-science simply because they believe in creation or question evolution.

It is important to distinguish strawman arguments from legitimate reductio arguments. Reductio argument reduces an argument down to premises, often to show inconsistency. Its most famous form, reductio ad absurdum, reduces an argument down to its components to show that while it may have seemed reasonable, it is absurd. At times, such valid arguments are incorrectly labeled strawman arguments, the difference between them being how accurately an argument is broken down.

For example, in chapter one, I used a type of reductio argument to question the belief that all morality is relative; there are no moral absolutes. If there are no moral absolutes, just preferences, then torturing babies for fun is not absolutely wrong; it is just a preference. Someone could claim this was just a strawman argument since the original argument was not about babies. Whether or not this is a Strawman argument would depend on the validity of the reductio argument. In this case, the reduction is valid. If there are no absolutes, there cannot be an absolute about torturing babies.

CIRCULAR REASONING (BEGGING THE QUESTION)

Circular reasoning is just like it sounds; you reason in a circle. Christians fall into this trap when they argue for the existence of God based on the Bible. The reason the Bible has authority for Christians is that they believe God inspired it. For it to be inspired by God, God must exist. As a result, an implied premise of this claim is that God exists, which is the very conclusion these Christians seek to prove. Arguing for God's existence based on the Bible's statements that say God exists is to argue in a circle.

Another example occurred in a discussion I had over the origin of life. I cited some of the evidence against the theory that life's origin was just a random event. Instead, it was the result of intelligent design.[43] The person I was discussing with, call him John, rejected any appeal to intelligent design as unscientific. I asked how this was different than an archaeologist finding a bowl and concluding it was the result of intelligent design? John's response was, "find an artifact, look for a creator, find a natural object, look for a natural process." I pointed out this begged the question and asked how one knows life is a "natural object?" His response was, "Natural objects are objects resulting from natural processes." So, in short, he rejected that life could be the result of intelligent design because it was a natural process. And we know it was a natural process because it

---

43   See Hushbeck, *Evidence for the Bible*, pp. 93-102

is a natural object. We know it was a natural object because it had a natural process. Completely circular.

A key distinction should be made here in terms of circular arguments and arguments that can be made in different directions. One type of argument is called the hypothetical syllogism. One of its variations follows the pattern, "If and only if A then B," or alternatively, "If not A then not B." When such an argument is sound, it is completely valid to reverse this argument, in which case it becomes "B, therefore A."

It is possible to argue that without God, there is no such thing as objective morality.[44] On the other hand, you can reverse this argument and argue that if there is an objective morality, then there must be a God. While these arguments are related, they are not circular. In fact, it is possible to accept the first argument that without God, there can be no objective morality and still reject God's existence. To do this, one would only have to reject the existence of objective morality. In short, one could believe that you could only have an objective morality with God and still reject there is objective morality. So there is no circularity here. To be circular, the conclusion must be part of the premises.

MISPLACED AUTHORITY

No one has the time and resources to research everything for themselves. A large part of everyone's beliefs is the statements and conclusions of those we consider authorities. Appealing to authorities is nothing more than a shortcut way of evaluating the evidence. Instead of undertaking an independent review of the evidence yourself, you rely on the work of others. This is normal and good. It is how knowledge grows generation after generation.

Christians do this at many levels every time they read a translation of the Bible. They are trusting in the work of others when they read John 1:1, "In the beginning was the Word, and the Word was with God, and the Word was God." Unless they can read Koine

---

44   See Hushbeck, *Christianity and Secularism*, pp. 173-181

Greek, the Greek of the first century, they trust this is a good translation of what John wrote. I would argue it is very reasonable to believe this. The evidence is so strong it would be irrational to question this in any meaningful way. Still, there is an appeal to authority.

You could, for example, learn to read the Greek of the first century and read this passage directly, Ἐν ἀρχῇ ἦν ὁ Λόγος, καὶ ὁ Λόγος ἦν πρὸς τὸν Θεόν, καὶ Θεὸς ἦν ὁ Λόγος. Even if you did, how do you know your knowledge of Greek is correct? A lot of our knowledge of first-century Greek comes from numerous scholars working for many years. While in theory, you could research all of this yourself, in reality, there simply is not enough time in a single lifetime, or even in many lifetimes, to learn everything. At some point, we all depend on authorities.

Arguments from authorities come in two forms. The first is an absolute argument that says: Position X is true because _____ says it is true. The problem with such arguments is that often authorities disagree. Those who disagree with you are very likely to cite different authorities that support them. Before long, one quickly finds themselves in a battle of 'my authorities are better than your authorities' – a battle which goes nowhere. At this point, the shortcut of appealing to authorities does not work. The discussion must either end or examine the evidence and reasoning that led these authorities to their respective conclusions.

The other type of authority argument is to establish the legitimacy of a given position. I have often run into people who deem it impossible to take the Bible seriously as a reliable document. Citing the many scholars (authorities) who believe it is a reliable document may not in and of itself establish that the Bible is a reliable document. Still, doing so does demonstrate this is a legitimate position. It is a position that cannot just be written off in the same way one might automatically reject those who claimed the earth is flat.

Both of the above are proper uses of authority. The fallacy of misplaced authority comes into play when the person cited is not an authority in the area under discussion. Often the people cited are authorities in other areas. For example, to cite Stephen Hawkings as an authority on cosmology, the area where he studied, worked, and is recognized as an authority, is legitimate. Citing him as an authority on religion is not.

Making this difficult is people do not restrict their comments to areas where they are authorities, nor is there any reason they should. For example, Hawkings has written about the implications his work in cosmology has on beliefs concerning God and creation. Because of his stature in cosmology, the implications he raises become a part of the debate. This is all well and good as long as we are not asked to accept his views concerning God because he is an authority. To do so would be the fallacy of Misplaced Authority.

We should not automatically accept Hawking's arguments concerning God and religion based on his being an authority in cosmology; neither should we automatically reject them. To automatically reject them because he was not an authority would be a form of ad hominem attack. The key is that we cannot take any short cuts by assuming these people have any special insight or knowledge. These augments are to be considered on their merits, not because these persons are authorities.

NON-SEQUITUR

Non-Sequitur arguments are those where the conclusion does not follow from the premises given. In many ways, Non-Sequitur, as a label, could apply for all errors in reasoning. As a stand-alone term, it normally comes into play where the argument is so strange it is impossible to see how the person got from their premises to their conclusion. As such, their actual error is difficult to see, so the generic Non-Sequitur is used.

Sometimes non-sequitur arguments are just the result of assuming or skipping over steps in the argument. Fixing the problem is just a matter of filling in the missing steps. But when no logical connection between the premise and the conclusion is apparent, and the person making the argument cannot explain the relationship, the argument is a non-sequitur.

RED HERRING

A Red Herring is a diversionary tactic to try and change the subject. Sometimes the change is to a related topic. Sometimes the change is to a completely different topic. Yet, at its core, a Red Herring attempts to avoid an argument by changing the topic. A common Red Herring when dealing with topics like the historical reliability of the Bible is suddenly to raise the subject of the Inquisition or the question of slavery in the Bible. The question of the accuracy of the Bible's depictions of events is different from the question of the Bible's moral view of slavery, which is different from the question of the Catholic Church's action during the Inquisition.

There is an important caveat here. While jumping from one to another would be a fallacy in a formal debate, most normal conversations are very dynamic and free-flowing. Thus, it can be difficult to tell a red herring from the normal changes in the topic. Such changes can and normally do occur in a casual discussion. Because of this, it is best to let many of these simply pass by without comment. Still, if you find yourself in a discussion dealing with a series of topic changes without ever reaching any conclusion, you may be dealing with red herrings.

CHALLENGE TO PROVE A NEGATIVE

A common but fallacious defense is a challenge to prove something didn't happen or isn't the case. Some Christians fall into this fallacy when talking with atheists, and they make a demand along the line of "Prove that God does not exist." That an atheist cannot prove God does not exist says absolutely nothing about the existence of God. The reason is that it is impossible to prove God does not exist. There are all kinds of things we cannot disprove. We cannot disprove something so silly as the claim that little green men who live on the moon cause cancer. But that we cannot disprove it does not mean that it is true, or even that it is rational to hold such a position.

Sometimes this is summarized as "you cannot prove a negative," but this is not strictly true. A lot in this statement depends on the precise definition of proof. There are also special cases where it is possible to prove a negative. A scientific test for the presence of oxygen could prove there was no oxygen in a given location. Yet, that it is sometimes possible to prove a negative does not mean that it is always possible to do so.

In the case of the question of the existence of God, just what type of evidence would show there is no God? What is the atheist expected to do when making this proof?

To see the problem, consider the following.

- God either exists, or he does not exist.
- If God exists, the atheist will not be able to prove God does not exist.
- If God does not exist, the atheist will still be unable to prove he does not exist.

Therefore, the fact the atheist cannot prove God does not exist tells us absolutely nothing about God's existence. A challenge to prove a negative becomes a fallacy when it is irrational.

ARGUING FROM IGNORANCE

Arguments from ignorance are little more than speculation. They occur when a conclusion is based not on the evidence but on the lack of evidence. In the last fallacy, we said that it is fallacious for a theist to argue that since the atheist cannot disprove God's existence, God must exist. Yet, it is equally fallacious for atheists to argue that since the theist cannot prove God's existence, God must not exist. In short, the absence of evidence does not automatically become evidence of absence.

The important word here is 'automatically.' There are exceptions to this fallacy, which involves the evidence's likelihood. When there should be evidence for a claim to be true, then the lack of evidence does serve as a reason to reject that claim. Someone claims a tornado swept through the center of your town. Still, when you went into town, everything seemed normal; the absence of any destruction would be a valid reason to question there had been a tornado.

Jesus was using a form of this argument in John 10:37 when he said: "Do not believe me unless I do what my Father does." God does not come in secret. If someone truly were the Son of God, they should be accompanied by miraculous signs and wonders as evidence of who they were. If Jesus had claimed to be the Son of God, but without any miracles, He would have been like a false prophet, claiming to speak for God without any supporting evidence. A lack of miracles would have been strong evidence to reject him, for such signs are to be expected.

The reason this becomes valid is apparent when putting these arguments into standard form. Normally, arguments from ignorance take the following form:

> There is no evidence to support A
> Therefore A is false

The argument above commits the fallacy of arguing from ignorance. Still, like many fallacies, this can be fixed by modifying the argument and adding a new premise:

> If A were true, we would have evidence to support it
> There is no evidence to support A
> Therefore A is false.

Atheists essentially make this argument when they demand proof of God's existence.

> If God exists, theists would be able to prove it.
> Theists cannot prove God exists
> Therefore God does not exist.

While the structure of this argument is valid, the argument remains unsound for two reasons. The first premise, "If God exists, theists would be able to prove it," is questionable at best. Still, the real problem with this argument is the use of the word "prove."

The term 'proof' is flexible and changes based on the context. It has a different meaning in mathematics than in a criminal court, which is different from a civil court. In an absolute sense, nothing can be strictly proven. As philosophers have pointed out, even Descartes's famous starting point of "I think; therefore I am" fails in a strict sense. It fails because it only shows that thinking is occurring, not an "I" thinking. When it comes to common usage, 'proof' is just the level of evidence required to determine whether something is true. Thus it changes meaning from person to person and from situation to situation.

Since the atheist argument is ambiguous over what constitutes proof, I take one of two approaches when confronted with this demand. The first is to ask for an exact definition for 'proof.' Defining 'proof' is often difficult to do. The few times any have attempted to define what they would consider proof, the results have either been inconsistent with what we know about God or have been impossible. Some have wanted God to appear to the world and perform miracles to show he is God, but that is not how God acts.

In the Hebrew Scriptures, God did, at times, intervene in miraculous ways for specific reasons. The same can be said of the New Testament. But it is also clear that these are few and far between and not the norm. Others ask for some sort of lab experiment showing God exists. What sort of experiment would this be? In short, they ask the impossible. Asking for the impossible is not a rational basis for rejecting God's existence when the impossible does not happen. Thus their demands are little better than the theist demanding atheists prove God does not exist.

The other approach I take is to reject the use of the word "proof" for the reasons stated above and instead use the word 'evidence.' In doing this, the first premise becomes, "if God exists, theists would be able to show evidence for it." This is a much more reasonable standard and fairly easy to demonstrate, as in this series's first two books. Usually, at this point, the atheist either directly or indirectly retreats to the concept of proof. Often with claims that the evidence is not evidence for God's existence because it does not show (prove?) that God exists.

The key point here is we should reject any argument based on a lack of evidence unless there is a reasonable expectation there would be evidence.

HASTY GENERALIZATION

Hasty generalization occurs whenever a conclusion about a few is transferred to the whole. Stereotypes are a good example of hasty generalizations. This category is difficult because, as the name implies, not all generalizations are bad, only the hasty ones. The generalization that "Christians believe that a god exists" would be a legitimate generalization about Christians. However, after seeing some Southern Baptists, you conclude that "Christians believe in baptism by immersion" that would be a hasty generalization, for not all Christians believe this.

Thus the real question is: when is a generalization justified? The simple answer is: when the evidence and the context support it. A common misconception is that all generalizations are bad, and any exception to a generalization invalidates the generalization. Yet this confuses a generalization with an absolute. It is a valid generalization to say that Christians believe God exists. Yet, if taken as an absolute, the statement is false. For example, there is a small number of people that follow Christian atheism. This movement follows some of the moral aspects of Christianity while rejecting the supernatural components. Still, Christian atheism is a very small group. Their existence does not invalidate the generalization that Christians believe that there is a God.

In many respects, hasty generalizations are inevitable, for the very reason that we do not know everything about everything. Our knowledge comes from our experience and authority, i.e., what others have told us. Christianity is a vast worldwide movement divided into many groups with a variety of beliefs. There is a core that unities them,[45] but there is also a wide range of beliefs where they differ.

A history professor of mine once told of a hasty generalization he had made about Christians. He was visiting Africa when some missionaries from Europe invited him over for lunch after church. My professor had grown up in America, and all the Christians he had known growing up did not drink alcohol. Thus he was shocked when he arrived, and the missionaries offered him a Gin and Tonic.

The real question with hasty generalization is what to do when challenged. Do you hold on tight to your belief despite the evidence, or do you realize your error? My history professor realized the sample size of the Christians he grew up with was too restrictive to maintain his belief that Christians did not drink alcohol. I have run into others who hold on to their beliefs despite growing evidence to the contrary. Perhaps this itself is a hasty generalization, but it has been my experience people tend to hold on to negative hasty generalizations more than positive ones.

FALSE CAUSE (POST HOC ERGO PROPTER HOC)

Outside of the subatomic world, we live in a universe governed by cause and effect. By definition, the cause of an event must precede the event. The False Cause fallacy occurs when we conclude that something caused an event because it happened before an event. Post hoc ergo propter hoc is Latin for "before a thing, therefore, caused a thing." One area where this often occurs is in religious discussions about God's approval or disapproval. In a general form, these arguments go as follows: you did X, and then something good/bad happened, and this showed God approves/disapproves of what you did.

A classic example of this fallacy occurs in the arguments of some who believe the KJV is the only word of God. One of the

---

45   Elgin L Hushbeck, Jr, *Christianity: The Basics* (Gonzales, FL: Energion, 2017)

arguments they use is that God blessed only the KJV. They argue England became a great nation after the KJV was translated and fell from greatness after the English people began using other translations. Now historians could undoubtedly come up with many other reasons leading to England's rise and fall as a great world power and would undoubtedly see England's rise beginning before the translation of the KJV. Just because this loosely corresponds to when the KJV was popular does not mean that God was blessing England because of the KJV.

There is also an additional problem. Following WWII, when England ceased to be a "great power," America took its place. Yet, America also used "other translations." The key point here is that to show a cause and effect relationship, you must do more than demonstrate the alleged cause occurred before the effect. You have to show there actually was a causal relationship going beyond a mere sequence in time.

BLACK OR WHITE / FALSE DILEMMA

The Black and White fallacy occurs when incorrectly framing an issue as a choice between two positions with no middle ground or other options. This results in a false choice to demonstrate one's position; one only needs to show the other position is false. If the correct choice is either Red or Green, it has to be Green if it is not Red. As a result, those using this type of argument often focus more on attacking the opposing position than supporting their own.

Now it is legitimate to argue based on elimination, which is called a disjunctive syllogism. A disjunctive syllogism is, for example, the type of argument I often use to demonstrate the Trinity.[46] Correctly done, you must consider all of the possible options. If the possible options are Red, Green, and Blue, only looking at Red and Green is a problem. If you don't consider all the options, then you fall into the fallacy of Black and White.

---

46 See *Christianity and Secularism*, pp. 78-84

This fallacy often occurs in the discussions concerning origins among both Christians and atheists. For some Christians and atheists, this is a choice between a completely supernatural literal-seven-day creation and a completely natural event that did not involve God in any way. No other options are considered. This fallacy is why it is common to see Christians attacking evolution as evidence against the Big Bang even though the Big Bang deals with the origin of the universe, while evolution deals with the origin of new forms of life. They are not even in the same branch of sciences.

For Christians caught up in this fallacy, there are only two positions, theirs and the opposition. Both the Big Bang and evolution are components of the opposing theories they reject. They falsely believe that to refute any part of the alternative view is the same as refuting all of the alternate view. As such, to demonstrate a problem with evolution is to demonstrate a problem with the Big Bang.

Of course, the problem with this reasoning is that there are more than two theories concerning origins. Even if one were to accept these Christians' arguments concerning evolution, it does not follow that the Big Bang theory is also wrong. Nor does it automatically follow that a literal 7-day creation is correct. There are other options. Thus the key to the Black and White argument is the possible conclusions are falsely restricted.

EQUIVOCATION

Language is how all discussions take place, and it works because there is an agreement as to what certain words used in certain contexts mean. Equivocation occurs when the language is modified improperly to make the argument. Consider the following question, "How many Gospels are in the Bible?" This seemingly simple question can actually have several possible and different correct answers, depending on what is meant by the word 'Gospel.'

First, one could take the word 'Gospel' as referring to books of the Bible, in which case the answer would be four, Matthew, Mark, Luke, and John. One could take, 'Gospel' as referring to the message of salvation brought by Jesus Christ, in which case there is only one. Finally, one could take 'gospel' as referring to any message of salvation, whether true or not, in which case there are several. It is used in this fashion in Galatians 1:9, "If anyone proclaims to you a gospel contrary to what you received, let that person be condemned!" Thus because of the ambiguity in the word 'gospel,' there are at least three possible correct answers to this question.

The rational response to such ambiguities is to seek greater clarification. Simply clarifying the intended meaning is all that should be required when someone is not sure. When responding based on a meaning different than intended, again, clarifying the intended meaning is all that should be required.

Equivocation enters into the picture when the different meanings of words are blurred. Equivocation can either be intentional or unintentional. A humorous example of this fallacy is the statement, "Our Pastor is a very responsible person; when anything goes wrong, he is responsible."

Equivocation is central to discussions concerning evolution and creation, for both of these words have several different possible meanings. Often in discussions, it is not clear which meaning is intended. Not only do the meanings of these words vary from person to person, but I have also encountered people who change their definitions from one minute to the next without warning.

In one discussion I had, an evolutionist kept rejecting all questioning of evolution by proclaiming that evolution was a fact. I asked him to define what he meant by evolution. He cited a textbook that defined evolution as the change in genes over time. Genes do change over time. If defined in this way, evolution is a fact. However, evolution is normally considered to more than just a change in genes. Genes change from person to person and over time from generation to generation. As a result, this definition did not cover most of his earlier claims concerning evolution, such as evolution being the mechanism for the emergence of new forms of life. He admitted this was true. What about all those other uses?

He said he had been referring to the theory of evolution instead of the fact of evolution.

The key to equivocation is language, not so much as a means of communication but as a barrier. It is the distortion of language to make an argument seem more reasonable than it is.

CONCLUSION

As we have seen in this section, there are a great many ways to reach invalid conclusions. This is not by any means a complete list but rather are just some of the more common fallacies. The errors detailed in this section do not come only from religious discussions. They come at us daily from a multitude of sources, from the advertising found on TV to the great works of literature. They are not confined to the uneducated but occurs in the arguments of great philosophers, scientist, historians, and theologians. We all stumble into using them from time to time. Our only defense against such error is to have a critical mind and analyze the arguments made to see if they are valid and if the premises support the conclusion. In short, the words of Paul are a pretty good guide: "Test everything, hold on to the good."

PART III
LIVING FAITH

CHAPTER 8

SEEKING
TRUTH

Jesus told him, "I am the way, the truth, and the life. No one comes to the Father except through me. If you have known me, you will also know my Father. From now on you know him and have seen him."
(John 14:6-7)

We live in a time of increasing polarization where people are withdrawing into ever-tightening circles. We increasingly group ourselves by politics, faith, and other beliefs not only with our friends but with our information sources. This polarization has been happening for a long time and is by no means restricted to religion. But it does include religion, and for many Christians, it started with a simple pulling back, away from the more uncomfortable aspects common in society.

There has always been a strong monastic trend within Christianity. A desire, not just to go on retreat, but to stay there. In the early days of Christianity, people would retreat to caves or live on top of a pillar for a few more publicly minded. During the Middle Ages, this impulse to withdraw became institutionalized into Monasteries with formal rules of conduct. This impulse has never gone away and reappeared in the early part of the 20th century.

Many years of controversy and debate with the emerging secular view of science and society culminated in the Scopes Trial in 1925. Whether that was the cause or not, following the trial, many Christians again began following this impulse, withdrawing from the public square. It was not that hard. After all, society was generally in agreement with Christian values. It was just easier not to have all the controversy.

There is a reason we are called to be both salt and light. Within less than a century, we have gone from living in a society that was generally accepting of Judeo-Christian values to one that is beginning to become hostile. We have gone from a position where Christians were called upon to be tolerant to seeking tolerance. The desire to opt-out of society cut both ways. Too many did not resist what they should have, such as the growing coarsening and secularization of society. Too many did not take a stand when they should, the most glaring example being evangelical's absence from the Civil Rights movement.

Sure there were exceptions; there were those who were the voices crying in the wilderness. But too many Christians were content simply to go to Church, maybe a mid-week Bible study; they were content to read Christian books, books bought at the Christian books store. As schools got bad, they were content to send their kids to a Christian school and maybe even a Christian College. Far too many Christians ignore politics and the culture as much as possible. Instead, they sought to insulate themselves from the corruption of the world.

Now, as we approach the 100th anniversary of the great retreat, Europe is in a Post Christian era. America is rapidly following as the broader culture is turning increasingly hostile and intolerant. Once Christians and Christian organizations were held up as examples to follow, we now have a culture where Christian organizations such as Focus on the Family are labeled Hate Groups. Today, Jesus' words pose a major challenge for the Church.

> "You are the salt of the world. But if the salt should lose its taste, how can it be made salty again? It's good for nothing but to be thrown out and trampled on by people. (Matthew 5:13)

Becoming Salty

A common response would be to band together and start a movement to "take back" the culture, but that is not how God works. Barring an exception that I will discuss later, God works through individuals, not groups. He asks us to examine ourselves, not point fingers at others. So rather than looking outwards for a solution, God challenges us to look inwards. Rather than pointing at others who are 'not living right,' God wants us to ask, 'How am I living?" In short, what is your faith? This is not asking what religion you belong to or even which Church you attend.

There are three aspects to the question of faith. The first is what; what do you believe? Most Christians would say they believe in Jesus Christ, but what do you believe about Christ, the church, the Bible. The second question is why; why do you believe what you believe? Why are you a Christian? Why do you go to Church? While there are certainly social aspects with attending Church, is there anything more than social reasons? If so, what is it? Finally, how; how does this affect your life? What do you do, or not do, because of your beliefs? How has it changed you?

Many Christians do not like the last question, as it seems to imply that one must work for their salvation. This concern, however, gets things backward, at least from a Christian point of view. As Paul wrote to the Ephesians,

> For by such grace you have been saved through faith. This does not come from you; it is the gift of God and not the result of actions, to put a stop to all boasting. For we are God's masterpiece, created in the Messiah Jesus to perform good actions that God prepared long ago to be our way of life. (Ephesians 2: 8-10)

As this passage says, we are saved by grace through faith, but it also says that we are created to "perform good actions." Christians do not work to earn salvation; their salvation is why they work. Christianity teaches that Jesus died for our sins, that by grace, we have eternal life, and that as a result, the Holy Spirit dwells within us. If someone really believed this, I mean really believed this; it should impact how they live their lives. As discussed in Part One, this is your faith; your beliefs put into action.

So what is your faith, and why do you believe it? These are very good questions for prayer, and the answer should be more than just a doctrinal statement. Consider, for example, a person's love for their spouse. If you asked them who their spouse is and why they love them, would you expect a description that sounded like a doctrinal statement?

Do not take these comments as a criticism of doctrinal statements. They are a great way to summarize what a group believes. They are also valuable for summarizing what you believe. They are important and useful, but they do not go to the heart of the question here. A doctrinal statement can play a vital role in what you believe about God, but it is not necessary.

The question of 'why' can be a difficult one. This question can be downright unsettling, particularly if you have never thought about your faith in this fashion before. The reason for this uneasiness is the possibility you are wrong lurks in the background. This uneasiness is something I often see when teaching apologetics. Having never been exposed to critics' arguments, hearing them for the first time can be unsettling, at least until considering the response. One side of an argument can often seem convincing until the other side is presented. Perhaps this is the reason some find it so easy to demonize their opponent or create strawman arguments. They cannot unsettle anyone if they are never taken seriously in the first place.

You have nothing to fear if your faith is correctly placed; if not, you still have nothing to fear, for any correction will only bring you closer to the truth. Assuming, of course, truth is your goal. There is a good chance you may discover you have had other goals driving your actions if you have never thought and prayed about your beliefs in this fashion. You may discover you need to reorient some of your beliefs or priorities. That is fine. In fact, it would be surprising if you didn't, for this would be saying you have everything perfect.

Nor is this a one-and-done process. Seeking a relationship with God that is grounded in truth is not something you ever finish. Salvation comes at the moment of conversion, but that is just the beginning of being made holy, the process of sanctification. There is a reason Paul speaks of the Church as the bride of Christ. While man and woman can become husband and wife in a moment, the process of the two becoming one is never complete. Likewise, the process of becoming more like Christ is a process that will never end.

THE WHAT

In one respect, there is only one correct answer to the question, what do you believe about God? Not enough. After all, God is infinite; we are finite. How could we ever hope to have a complete understanding of God? Thus, a common experience when learning about God is realizing how much you do not know. Put another way, how much there is still left to know?

Some learn the basics, and thinking that is enough, stop. As one aphorism puts it, the greatest obstacle to learning is the illusion of knowledge. The writer of Hebrews addressed a form of this when he wrote,

> On this topic we have much to say and it is difficult to explain, since you have become sluggish in hearing. For though you should in fact be teachers by this time, you need someone to teach you the beginning elements of God's utterances. You have gone back to needing milk, not solid food. For everyone who lives on milk is inexperienced in the message of righteousness, because he is an infant. But solid food is for the mature, whose perceptions are trained by practice to discern both good and evil. Therefore we must progress beyond the elementary instructions about Christ and move on to maturity, not laying this foundation again: repentance from dead works and faith in God, teaching about ritual washings, laying on of hands, resurrection of the dead, and eternal judgment. (Hebrews 5:11-6:3)

What do you do if you find yourself in this camp? In this, as in so many things, the first step is prayer. After all, how can you expect to learn more about God if you do not talk to Him? Seek God's help, His guidance. Ask Him to reveal the gaps in your understanding and ways to fill them. Make prayer an integral part of your life as you seek a deeper understanding of God.

The next step is God's word. Read it. Of course, this immediately raises the question of which translation. If you are new enough to reading the Bible that you need to ask the question, then choosing one can be a bit overwhelming. The first question you need to answer is: Which kind of translation do you want? There are generally two types of translations: Literal and Idiomatic. When translating a given passage, the differences in grammar and sentence structure between languages make a straight word for word translation impractical in most cases. For example, a straight word for word translation of 1 John 5:20 would read:

> we know and that the son of the god is come and has given to us understanding in order that we might know the true and we are in the true in the son of him jesus christ this is the true god and life eternal

While it is possible to understand what the apostle John is saying, it is a little difficult to read and can be confusing. In fact, a word for word translation could be misleading or even wrong because of the differences in grammar and word order.[47] A straight word for word translation also loses the character of the original language. The Bible is not only the word of God; it is great literature.

A literal translation tries to stay as close to a word-for-word translation as possible while retaining its readability. A good example of a literal translation would be the New American Standard Bible (NASB). The NASB translates 1 John 5:20 as :

---

47   A double negative (not nothing) become a positive in English(not
     nothing = something) In Greek a double negative is use for emphasis.
     (not nothing = absolutly nothing).

> We know that the Son of God has come and has given us understanding in order that we might know Him who is true; and we are in Him who is true, in His Son Jesus Christ. This is the true God and eternal life.

The King James Version, also a literal translation, translates 1 John 5:20 as:

> And we know that the Son of God is come, and hath given us an understanding, that we may know him that is true, and we are in him that is true, even in his Son Jesus Christ. This is the true God, and eternal life.

On the other hand, while striving for accuracy, an idiomatic translation attempts to preserve the text's overall flow and beauty. An example of an idiomatic translation would be the New International Version (NIV). The NIV translates 1 John 5:20 as:

> We know also that the Son of God has come and has given us understanding, so that we may know him who is true. And we are in him who is true -- even in his Son Jesus Christ. He is the true God and eternal life.

As you can see, both the Idiomatic and Literal translations are faithful to the Bible's original text. Some people like literal translations because they want to be as close to the original text as possible without learning Greek and Hebrew. (Then again, some do learn Greek and Hebrew.) Others prefer idiomatic translations because they find them easier to read and understand. Get and use both types if you can afford it – both have their strengths and weaknesses. Among the major Bible versions, there really are no bad translations. If your church uses a particular version, that would be a good choice. When choosing a Bible, a major consideration should be: Is this a Bible that you will read and study? Purchasing a Bible is a waste of money unless you read it and study it. There are also many websites with a range of translations you can use for free.

Even with a good translation, understanding the Bible can be difficult. While you may be reading a translation in modern

English, the text underlying the translation was written by and for people living thousands of years ago. It was a different time with a different culture. At times, the Bible makes references, which would have been clear to the people who first read the text but would be unknown to the average person today.

The Bible frequently speaks to people where they are, pointing them to where they should be. As a result, living in a civilization influenced for thousands of years by the Bible, things can appear very different to us than they did to those to whom a given passage was written. A good example of this, Deuteronomy 21:18-21,

> "If a man has a stubborn son who does not obey his parents, and although they try to discipline him, he still refuses to pay attention to them, then his parents shall seize him and bring him before the elders at the gate of his city. Then they are to declare to the elders of their city: 'Our son is stubborn and rebellious. He does not obey us. He lives wildly and is a drunkard.' Then all the men of his city shall stone him with stones so that he dies. This is how you will remove this evil from among you. Then all Israel will hear of it and will be afraid."

Many are shocked by the idea that you should stone your children for disobedience. Many critics use this as a reason to reject the Bible as a whole, but that is viewing the passage in today's context, not the context of the time it was written. With any new rule or law, what changed is more important than what stayed the same. In the context of the period, a father's right to kill a child was the norm; to question it was to involve oneself in internal family matters that were none of your business.

This passage says no; you cannot just kill your child; you do not have that right. From now on, if you want your child killed, you must bring them before the elders at the gate. These elders served as a sort of law court for the community; they would pass judgment. Rather than saying you should stone your child, this passage removes that power from the family. It takes the power of life and death and transfers it to the community, where it remains today.

This law has become so ingrained into our culture that some question the need for it. After all, who would kill their own child? Sadly, it was needed and still is needed today in some parts of the world. The father's right to kill their children is still part of some cultures going under the name of honor killing. On the other hand, among the Jews following this law, there is no recorded instance of a child's execution in this fashion. Nor should this be surprising. It is one thing to get mad at a child and kill them. It is another thing entirely to go to the elders and justify why they should have your child executed. Not only is there plenty of time to cool down, what family wants such scrutiny?

This passage is a great example of why, while it is very important to read the Bible, you must also study it. It is important to know the background and context of the various books. Hopefully, you get some of this in the sermons of your church. We live at a time when it has never been easier to learn about the Bible. There are numerous books, websites, videos, podcasts on all aspects of the Bible from its languages, linguistics, archeology, history, cultural background, theology, and many other areas. Granted, not all of it is of the same quality; still, it is a strange paradox that when learning about the Bible has never been so easy and accessible, Biblical literacy is so low.

A word of caution, there are many good books written to help you study the Bible. There are so many that you could spend all your time reading and studying books about the Bible without ever reading or studying the Bible. You must be careful to allow God's Word to speak to you directly. Your first source for understanding the Bible should be the Bible, under the guidance of the Holy Spirit. As such, prayer must accompany Bible reading and study.

Bible reading and Bible study are matters requiring a lifelong commitment. Nobody ever knows enough about what the Bible says because, as the Word of God, it never ceases to speak. God can and does speak to our hearts through the Bible. Sometimes He speaks as we are reading. Sometimes He only speaks after we have studied and struggled with a particular passage for some time. The

Holy Spirit empowers the word of God. He uses it to mold us, change us, and conform us to his will. As the writer of Hebrews wrote:

> For the word of God is living and active, sharper than any double-edged sword, piercing until it divides soul and spirit, joints and marrow, as it judges the thoughts and purposes of the heart. (Hebrews 4:12).

We cannot spend a long time reading and studying the Bible without facing our own failings, our sinfulness. But as our sinfulness is revealed, so is the solution.

> How blessed is the person,
> who does not take the advice of the wicked,
> who does not stand on the path with sinners,
> and who does not sit in the seat of mockers.
> But he delights in the Lord's instruction,
> and meditates in his instruction day and night.
> (Psalms 1:1-2).

To understand a passage in the Bible, first, you must read the passage and seek what the original author was trying to say to the original audience. This is where the study part comes in. Only after you understand this should you ask the question, what does this mean for me? Throughout this process, we must be on our guard for all the problems, and errors discussed earlier in this book, for they are sure to creep in unannounced and unwanted.

THE BODY OF CHRIST

Thus far, I have been focusing on what you can do as an individual, but we are all fallen and fallible, prone to mistakes and errors. This is where others come in. We all make mistakes, but we do not make the same mistakes. Discussing with others is the best way to discover your mistakes while helping others discover theirs. Now I would not recommend that you run out and find a hardcore skeptic for your first discussion. Hopefully, there are people in your life you can talk to about God, your study, and what you are learning.

We can have discussions to seek the truth or confirm what we already believe. The latter is easy. Simply restrict your discussions to those you know already agree with your view. An alternate form of this approach is to ask many people and to keep asking until you get the answer you wanted from the start. Seeking confirmation is easy; seeking correction is hard. We should seek good honest discussions and discussions to seek the truth with those who can help correct us.

The other side of this problem is to be so open to correction that you become ungrounded. As Paul writes in Ephesians 4, God gave those to lead and teach us,

> until all of us are united in the faith and in the full knowledge of God's Son, and until we attain mature adulthood and the full standard of development in the Messiah. Then we will no longer be little children, tossed like waves and blown about by every wind of doctrine, by people's trickery, or by clever strategies that would lead us astray.

The first place we should seek guidance is from the leadership of our Church. There are, of course, the sermons, but hopefully, there are Bible studies as well. Bible studies where you can ask questions. In my Bible studies, I have two rules in this context.

1) Feel free to interrupt at any time. After all, anything you have to say will probably be more interesting than anything I will be saying.
2) Feel free to disagree with the instructor at any time. My goal is not to get you to agree with me. My goal is to get you to wrestle with the word of God and come to your own opinion.

In my classes, I teach books of the Bible, verse by verse, with a strong emphasis on literary structure and each verse's context. While I have notes, I have no fixed plan other than to pick up where I left off. Some weeks we cover up to 10 verses or more. At other times it can take a couple of weeks for a single verse. A few times, people have come with questions, and we spent the entire class discussing their questions.

I open each class with prayer and include as part of my prayer that the Holy Spirit will take the class where He wants it to go. I believe he does. Not because he is working through me, but because he works through the class. I said above that God works through individuals, not groups, but that there was an exception. This is the exception. God does work through us, all the believers that make up the body of Christ.

If you are new to Bible study, this type of study may be too in-depth. That is ok. One thing about the Bible is that its message is so simple a child can understand it. Yet, it is so profound that one can spend a lifetime and never fully explore its depths. So find a Bible study that matches your level and needs.

At some point, you will be well enough grounded in your church's teachings to begin to branch out in your discussion to those in other churches. The number of various churches is a testament to what extent Christians disagree. This is normal and ok. In Romans 14, Paul addressed disagreements that existed among believers in Rome. There were disagreements over what food one could eat and what day you should honor the Lord. Paul could have settled these issues by stating the correct view. He did this with food, saying, "Everything is clean." But he went on to say, "it is wrong to make another person stumble because of what you eat."

Paul describes the problem concerning special days as, "One person decides in favor of one day over another, while another person decides that all days are the same." Here Paul did not decide the issue, but rather simply said, "Let each one be fully convinced in his own mind." It is not clear whether the dispute concern a special observance or a dispute over the weekly observance. The latter is still with us today. Most churches have the main weekly observance on the Lord's Day, i.e., Sunday. However, a few believe this violates the commandment to "remember to keep the Sabbath day holy." Therefore, they worship on Saturday.

A difference over days would be a very good reason for Paul to settle this issue and settle it clearly. After all, how can the Church be unified if people cannot even agree on when they are to worship? Yet, surprisingly, Paul does not settle this issue. Instead, he says, "Each must be fully convinced in his own mind" (Romans 14:5). After discussing how we should do everything thing for the Lord, he concludes, "Therefore we must not pass judgment on one another, but rather determine never to place an obstacle or a trap before a brother or sister" (Romans 14:13).

If such disagreements are ok, and even the norm, how do we reconcile this with passages such as Ephesians 4:3-6?

> Do your best to maintain the unity of the Spirit by
> means of the bond of peace. There is one body and one Spir-
> it. Likewise, you were called to the one hope of your calling.
> There is one Lord, one faith, one baptism,
> one God and Father of all,
> who is above all, through all, and in all.

How can there be so many different churches if there is one body? Shouldn't we, like Joseph Smith, ask which church is the one True Church? The simple answer is no, and this question is grounded in a confusion between local churches and the universal Church.

The one true Church, the universal church, is composed of all believers. Like many of his letters, Paul wrote Ephesians to a local church, i.e., the believers in the city of Ephesus. Like most churches, this was one that had its issues, which Paul addressed in his letter. There were Jewish/Gentile tensions like many churches, but here the main problem seemed to be with Gentiles; they were boasting about their new status.

Because of this, Paul spends most of chapter one pointing out God's role in salvation, which is total, starting with how "he chose us in the Messiah before the creation of the universe" (Ephesians 1:4). In chapter two, he comes to our role in salvation, which was pretty dismal, "You used to be dead because of your offenses and sins" (Ephesians 2:1). Paul sums this up with, "For by such grace you have been saved through faith. This does not come from you; it is the gift of God and not the result of actions, to put a stop to all boasting" (Ephesians 2:8-9). In the next section, aimed primarily at the Gentiles, he then talks about how the two groups were brought together by Jesus,

> creating in himself one new humanity from the two, thereby making peace, and reconciling both groups to God in one body through the cross, on which he eliminated the hostility. He came and proclaimed peace for you who were far away and for you who were near. For through him, both of us have access to the Father by one Spirit. Ephesians 3:15-18

The church in Philippi was also a church split by disunity, and again Paul wrote to them about the importance of unity,

> The only thing that matters is that you continue to live as good citizens in a manner worthy of the gospel of the Messiah. Then, whether I come to see you or whether I stay away, I may hear all about you—that you are standing firm in one spirit, struggling with one mind for the faith of the gospel. Philippians 1:27

We are united in the Holy Spirit as the body of Christ, not unity for unity's sake, but unity for a specific cause; unity for the sake of the Gospel.

Seen in this light, Paul's reluctance to settle every little theological dispute makes sense. There was no way he could settle all of them, even for his day, much less the ones that would arise in the future. So he stressed a more important message: Don't let these disputes get in the way of the common task of the Gospel. As Christians, we can, will, and do disagree about a whole range of theological issues.

While Christians are united in the belief that Christ will return, there is a disagreement over the timing. Some believe he will come at the beginning of the tribulation, some around the middle or pre-wrath, while still others believe he will return at the end. While a clear difference of opinion, this is not a reason for disunity. At the church I attend, all three views are held by various members, and at least two of the views are represented by the pastoral staff. Yet while we disagree with one another, we are still worshiping together, and more importantly, working for the Gospel together.

While Christians can band together in groups, the Holy Spirit still works through us as individuals as our faith permits. Our faith is key here, for if we lack faith, we will resist the Holy Spirit. Intellectually, we know that God knows best and that His ways are better than our ways. And yet, our actions say something else. Often our actions say we know better; we know what really is important. The difference between what we say and believe to be true and what we do is our lack of faith.

This attitude comes into play in our interactions with other Christians. Some believe they are doing ok; their beliefs are correct, but they wonder about those in other churches. After all, if they were as close to God as I am, wouldn't they believe what I believe and attend the same church I do? Often such an attitude is not only self-centered, but it also demonstrates a lack of faith. It is a lack of faith that the Holy Spirit knows what He is doing as He works in the lives of others. It says you need to come in and set them straight.

If that is why you seek discussions with other Christians, i.e., to correct them, you are doing so for the wrong reason. There are many other and valid reasons to have discussions with other Christians concerning disagreements. You can discuss areas of disagreement to get a better understanding of what others believe and why. Gaining such an understanding will tend to break down barriers and build unity with the body as a whole. You can have discussions to get a better understanding of what you believe and why. This reason is a major factor for me. Personally, I have always found it much easier to study when focused on a particular question or issue.

Other Christians often raise issues and perspectives I had not considered before. These new considerations drive me back into the

Bible and prayer to understand how they fit into my understanding. Sometimes, I come away stronger in my belief; often, I come away with a more nuanced view; a few times, I ended up changing my view. If nothing else, I come away with a better understanding of why there is a disagreement. But, if done correctly and for the right reasons, it is always beneficial.

Perhaps you have the discussions simply because you enjoy examining such issues. It really does not matter as long as the ultimate goal is the search for truth. It results in greater unity of the Body in its propagation of the Gospel. Both are important. Some might argue that for the sake of unity, we should not discuss such things at all. Perhaps. But, while in some cases, this will be the correct choice, it is not the optimum choice, and it comes at the cost of truth.

THE VALUE OF ERROR

A major consideration in all of this is the question: Is it ok to be wrong? From childhood, we are taught no. We are pushed to get 100% on tests and straight A's in our classes in school. Often this is to the detriment of the very thing we are in school to do. Following a graduation ceremony once, a former student in her cap and gown came up to me. As I had taught her first class when she started back to college, I remembered her, and I was happy to see her graduate. I was a bit taken aback when she said she would have had a 4.0 except for my class. Surprisingly, she went on to thank me for it.

One of the standard things I would always talk about in such introductory classes was the importance of learning over grades or even a diploma. Grades and a diploma are important, but they will not get you the things you seek by going to school, such as a better job, more money, etc. The education you get, the things you learn are what are really important. Given an assignment where you could write about something you know, getting an easy A, or learning something new where you might only get a B, I always recommend learning something new. You are not in school to get good grades; you are in school to learn, and you should learn as much as you can.

This graduating student took that message to heart. Since she did not get an A in my class, the possibility of a 4.0-grade point average was already gone. She spent the rest of her time at college, focusing on learning. She said it was so liberating not to have to worry about getting an A. It was the first time I have ever been thanked for not giving someone an A.

While in discussions, we should likewise keep our attention on seeking truth, more than pointing out errors. This attitude is particularly true when dealing with those who are younger in the faith and not as knowledgeable. It is often far more valuable to give them something to consider and think about than a full analysis of where and why they are wrong. The latter is very likely to convince them it is unwise to share their point of view as it will only make them look foolish.

Giving them something to consider will encourage them to study and seek the truth. It also requires faith, faith that the Holy Spirit will guide them, and faith they will be willing to be led. We have to resist the temptation to do it ourselves and risk that they may conclude differently. In short, we must accept it is ok for them to be wrong. Let us hope that it is, for we just might be the ones in error.

This view, as it was with my student losing her 4.0-grade point average in the first class, it is very liberating. You are no longer responsible for what others think. That is between them and God. You are responsible for what you believe. You can engage in discussions with other Christians without any concern for winning or even if others are right. Your only concern is whether you are right; are you seeking the truth; are you building the unity of the body? This view does not mean that you do not care about them; only they are not your responsibility.

So far, we have been talking about discussions concerning non-essential beliefs, beliefs such as the exact timing, in relation to the tribulation, of Christ's return. These are beliefs about which Christians have disagreed. But there are other beliefs, core beliefs about God, Jesus Christ, Salvation, and the Bible that Christians have agreed on for 2000 years, be they Catholic, Protestant, or Orthodox. These beliefs define Christianity as a religion. I have a chapter discussing them in *Christianity and Secularism*.[48] An expanded version of that Chapter was published as *Christianity: The Basics*,[49] so I will not discuss them again here. Suffice it to say that these are the beliefs upon which the Body of Christ, guided by the Holy Spirit, agrees.

Disagreement about non-essential belief is ok, and as Paul said, "Each must be fully convinced in his own mind" (Romans 14:5). Paul had another view when it came to differences concerning core beliefs. "If anyone proclaims to you a gospel contrary to what you received, let that person be condemned!" (Galatians 1:9) Taking one side or the other on an issue where Christians disagree is one thing. Siding against the Body of Christ is another. Some argue the true Church was corrupted and cannot be trusted. Corruption certainly has happened down through the ages, so has reform.

Still, the amount of corruption required to change the core would involve a massive, and I would argue impossible, level of conspiracy. It would call into question the power of Jesus to establish his Church and the guidance of the Holy Spirit. It would say that the first time the Gospel failed; now it must be restored, and not just reformed. But any such second giving is precluded by Jude 1:3,

> Dear friends, although I was eager to write to you about the salvation we share, I found it necessary to write to you and urge you to continue your vigorous defense of the faith that was passed down to the saints once and for all.

While this is a good translation, this is one of the places where it is hard to get the Greek text's full impact. Greek is similar to

---

48   Hushbeck, *Christianity and Secularism*, pp. 67-91
49   Hushbeck, *Christianity: The Basics*

English in its use of adjectives where placement matters. To say *the boy is good* is weaker than saying *the good boy*. In Greek, when the adjective appears between the definite article (the) and the noun, as in *the good boy*, it indicates a defining quality. If we translate Jude's statement preserving the word order, the key part of what he wrote is, "the once and for all passed down to the saints faith." While awkward in English, it conveys that the true faith would only be given only one time.

Disagreements about the mode of Baptism (sprinkling or immersion) or the timing of Christ's return (pre, mid, or post tribulation) are legitimate disagreements between Christians. Disagree about the core, and you disagree with the Body of Christ. Does this mean the core is off-limits for discussion? Not at all. Everything is open for discussion. However, if you discuss a core belief, such as whether or not Jesus is God, you may not be talking to a Christian. At least not a Christian in any historical sense. You have gone beyond the body and are now influencing the world. In doing so, you are becoming salt and light.

BECOMING SALT AND LIGHT

In the verse immediately following Jesus' question and comment about salt, Jesus goes on to say,

> "You are the light of the world. A city located on a hill can't be hidden. People don't light a lamp and put it under a basket but on a lamp stand, and it gives light to everyone in the house. In the same way, let your light shine before people in such a way that they will see your good actions and glorify your Father in heaven." (Matthew 5:13-16)

We are to be both salt and light. From time to time, people have asked, 'Why doesn't God work in the world anymore?' 'Why are there no miracles?' I believe such questions are based on a false premise. God does work in the world today. He does so through believers, His body, and they assist in the greatest miracle of all, the transformation of a dead soul into a new life, the miracle of salvation. That is the heart of the Gospel.

I said above that our primary focus should be on us and what we can do, not pointing fingers at others. Our discussions should focus on seeking truth more than correcting the mistakes we see in others. This attitude is important when dealing with those in your church. It is also well and good when dealing with Christians from other churches and other denominations. But does it apply when dealing with the world at large? The basic answer is yes, and again it comes down to a matter of faith.

Our role is to live for Christ and to proclaim the Gospel. We have been granted the great privilege to be part of the process, but in the end, it is God who saves. Do you have faith in God to do his part? I have written elsewhere[50] that we all build walls to keep God out of our lives. As an apologist, my job is to help remove those walls, brick by brick, until there is nothing between the person and the Cross. At that point, my job ends. The rest is between the person and the Holy Spirit. One question is, do you have enough faith in God to do his part?

I learned very quickly that a large part of what I do as an apologist is to explain why Christians do not always act as they should. Some of this is a "bad rap," and some justified. Concerning the part that is justified, some of it stems from Christians who break God's laws, such as a pastor caught up in a sex scandal. But some of it is people acting hatefully under the guise of defending God. In my book *Doing Apologetics*, I write about some visiting evangelists who came to a secular college I was attending. They would condemn people with hateful language for not following God.[51] When I asked about their tactics, they said it was needed to get attention. Once they had their attention, they could proclaim the truth.

For me, this showed a lack of faith. Our job is to proclaim the Gospel. One of the key verses for apologetics is 1 Peter 3:15. It is often quoted as, "Be prepared to give a defense to everyone who

50   Elgin L Hushbeck, Jr, *Doing Apologetics* (Gonzales, FL: Energion, 2019)
51   Hushbeck, *Doing Apologetics*, pp. 8-9.

asks you to explain the hope you have." Some take this to mean we should be ready with things like the latest archeology and scientific evidence to answer any critics we encounter. But that is not really what Peter is saying.

In the part of the letter leading up to this point, Peter discusses the great mercy of God in granting "us a new birth resulting in an immortal hope" (1 Peter 1:3). He calls for us to be Holy (1:15-16) and to "…rid yourselves of every kind of evil and deception, hypocrisy, jealousy, and every kind of slander" (2:1). We must submit ourselves to our rulers and those in authority over us and to "suffer patiently when wronged" (2:19) for "the Messiah also suffered for you" (v 2:21). Peter sums this up, saying,

> Finally, all of you must live in harmony, be sympathetic, love as brothers, and be compassionate and humble. Do not pay others back evil for evil or insult for insult. Instead, keep blessing them, because you were called to inherit a blessing.

He is talking about being holy and suffering for God. It is in this context of suffering that 1 Peter 3:15 appears. Here is the verse in the broader context,

> Who will harm you if you are devoted to doing what is good? But even if you should suffer for doing what is right, you are blessed. "Never be afraid of their threats, and never get upset. Instead, exalt the Messiah" as Lord in your lives. Always be prepared to give a defense to everyone who asks you to explain the hope you have. But do this gently and respectfully, keeping a clear conscience, so that those who speak evil of your good conduct in the Messiah will be ashamed of slandering you. After all, if it is the will of God, it is better to suffer for doing right than for doing wrong. (1 Peter 3:13-17)

Rather than being ready for the challenge of a skeptic, the question Peter was expecting was more along the lines of, "how can you still have hope in the face of such suffering?" Peter challenges us to live in a way that attracts comments. It is a call to faith, to live out what you say you believe. Having talked about the great mercy God has shown us, dying for our sins so we can be made holy in him, Peter asks us to "live in harmony, be sympathetic, love as brothers, and be compassionate and humble" (2:21). When people ask about our hope, we are to answer them but to "do this gently and respectfully, keeping a clear conscience" (3:16)

Again, the focus here is on us and our conduct. This is a hard message. Peter is clear that the Christians to whom he was writing were being treated unjustly. He could have called on them to denounce the evil perpetrated against them. Yet he tells them, "...do not pay others back evil for evil or insult for insult. Instead, keep blessing them, because you were called to inherit a blessing" (3:9).

We are called to be both salt and light, but we do this by living out our faith. Some people struggle over whether or not to share their faith, and I have heard many sermons encouraging people to do so. We should proclaim the Gospel, but we have very little choice when it comes to being a witness for Christ. There is an old question about how you live: If Christianity were a crime, would there be enough evidence to convict you? The only way not to be a witness for Christ is to hide it so well that no one knows you are a Christian. You do not need to make a big deal about it. If being a Christian is an important part of your life, people who know you will know you are a Christian, just like they will know your hobbies, the type of Movie and TV shows you like, and other things about you.

If people know you are a Christian, you are a witness for Christ. The only other question is, what type of witness will you be? We proclaim our true faith by how we live our lives. We witness to others more by what we do than what we say. Paul, writing to the Galatians, said, "the fruit of the Spirit is love, joy, peace, patience, kindness, goodness, faithfulness, gentleness, and self-control." (5:21-22) Is that how you live? If your friends had to describe you, would they use words such as these?

We impact the world by living our lives as faithful followers of Christ. We should not withdraw from the culture but engage the culture. This will not always be easy. It is becoming increasingly harder as the broader culture turns more hostile. As we challenge the culture by how we choose to live, the culture will push back. Jesus is not only the way and the life; he is the truth. (John 14:6) As Christians, we must stand for the truth. Standing for the truth among a culture that has embraced lies will not be popular. The emerging hostility in the United States is nowhere near the persecution levels faced by Christians in some countries, but it is growing. Some have lost friends and family members. Some have lost their jobs or businesses.

Rod Dreher wrote in his book, *Live Not By Lies*, on the growing intolerance facing Christians. He sees parallels in the persecution faced by dissidents in Eastern European countries in the Cold War. He writes how "truth cannot be separated from tears. To live in truth requires accepting suffering."[52] It is a hard lesson. Particularly hard for Christians in post-Christian cultures, who are still used to how comfortable and easy this used to be. But it is the message we see in books such as James and 1 Peter. As Dreher sums up, "This is the cost of liberty. This is what it means to live in truth. There is no other way. There is no escape from the struggle. The price of liberty is eternal vigilance—first of all, over our own hearts."[53]

Voting is another vital way we impact the culture. Peter said, "For the Lord's sake, submit yourselves to every human authority: whether to the king as supreme or to governors who are sent by him to punish those who do wrong and to praise those who do right" (1 Peter 2:13-14). But what does this mean in a democratic form of government? What does this mean when the ultimate power resides with the people, not a King? Some resist voting because they don't like either candidate in an election. Here are three considerations. First, at least in the United States, we elect secular leaders, not religious ones. Second, God picked David to be King, though he was an adulterer and a murderer. Third, while many complain about the two-party system, that is what we currently have. Maybe

---

52 Rod Dreher, *Live Not by Lies: A Manual for Christian Dissidents,* (New York, Penguin Random House, 2020) p 212

53 Dreher, *Live,* p 212

in the future, it will change, but at the moment, that is what we have. As such, you can participate in the choice or leave it to others to decide for you.

Finally, you need to talk about what you believe. Not in any scripted monologue, but in a normal, natural way, just like you would talk about anything else that is important in your life. The discussion will not be all that different from the discussions mentioned earlier in this chapter. Your primary goal can still be seeking the truth. Even when I am talking to a hardcore atheist, I still try to be open to valid problems they might point out in my beliefs; I am still trying to learn. I am still seeking to come closer to the truth. In short, I still seek discussion rather than correction or condemnation. I can do this because I am confident in my beliefs and trusting in the Holy Spirit as I seek to live out my faith.

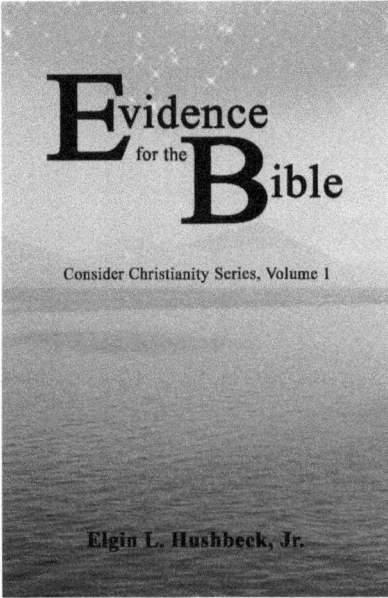

Evidence for the Bible

Consider Christianity Series, Volume 1

Elgin L. Hushbeck, Jr.

"Hushbeck is truly a present day champion in defense of Christianity and the Bible." Dr. Robert C. McKibben, retired United Methodist Pastor

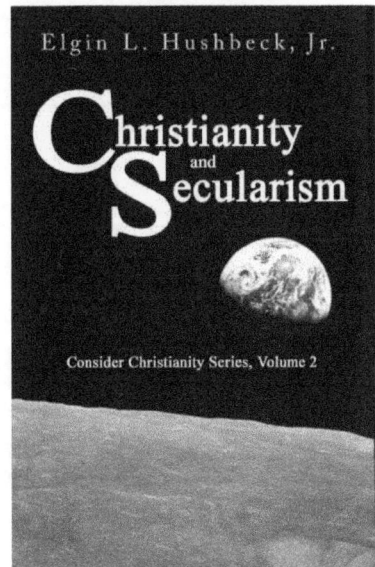

Elgin L. Hushbeck, Jr.

Christianity and Secularism

Consider Christianity Series, Volume 2

ELGIN L. HUSHBECK, JR.

DOING
APOLOGETICS

Topical
Line
Drives

Volume 36

Participatory Study Series

Σ

Just $5.99 (papberback) or $2.99 (ePub)

www.ingramcontent.com/pod-product-compliance
Lightning Source LLC
Chambersburg PA
CBHW021233090426
42740CB00006B/508

* 9 7 8 1 6 3 1 9 9 7 4 4 0 *